Seed Wars

That which has been is that which will be,
And that which has been done is that which will be done.
So there is nothing new under the sun.
Is there anything of which one might say,
"See this, it is new"?
Already it has existed for ages
Which were before us.
There is no remembrance of earlier things;
And also of the later things which will occur,
There will be for them no remembrance
Among those who will come later still.

            Ecclesiastes 1:9-11

Endorsements

Since Genesis 1, a battle has been raging between God's Seed and Lucifer's diabolical seed. That battle is now at a fever pitch. Indeed, cultural, racial, and ideological wars are escalating to determine who controls the souls of nations. Most of all, there is a desperate and passionate war being fought for the souls of human beings Jesus died for.

My friend Greg Hood and Scott Oatsvall do a masterful job of revealing the power of evil behind this. In this book, *Seed Wars*, Greg & Scott go back to ancient manuscripts, and the reason behind a race of giants that our heroes of faith faced and overcame is exposed. But far more than that…Greg and Scott reveal how we conquer giants in the land of our times. God's seed wins. The giants still fall. Get ready to be challenged. Get ready to fight. Get prepared to triumph.

Dr. Tim Sheets
Best Selling Author of *Angel Armies, Planting the Heavens*
Tim Sheets Ministries
The Oasis Church, Middletown, OH
www.TimSheets.org

The battle between mankind and the Nephilim has been raging for centuries. No, not in the conventional sense. There are no modern battlegrounds bloodied with fallen titans and valiant defenders. The battle is in the unseen realm—what we believe, and how we act upon it.

Regardless of what you believe about the sons of God and the daughters of men, Seed Wars illuminates with fresh perspective. Dr. Greg Hood and Dr. Scott Oatsvall have not written the definitive work on the subject. Rather, they have opened a door for the willing scholar to step through and engage the subject.

I encourage you to keep an open mind, a guarded heart, and a willing spirit to consider what the evidence suggests. And if need be, keep a nightlight burning in your bedroom.

Dr. Dutch Sheets
Dutch Sheets Ministries and *Give Him 15* daily prayer and decrees. Bestselling author of: A*uthority in Prayer, An Appeal to Heaven, Intercessory Prayer*
www.dutchsheets.org

Every believer is called, like Joshua, to defeat the giants. In modern spiritual warfare we have associated these giants with spiritual strongholds and issues we must gain victory over. However, in *Seed Wars*, our eyes are opened to the influence of the original giants, called the Nephilim in Genesis 6, on our world. What unfolds in these pages will cause you to look at scripture, and biblical history with new eyes, and to look to our future with greater discernment.

Jane Hamon
Author of *Dreams & Visions, Discernment, Declarations for Breakthrough* and *Confronting the Thief*

We need to go back to move forward. I believe the days ahead are prophetically outlined in the Book of Genesis, going all the way back to the Seed of woman and, of course, the serpent's seed. Greg Hood and Scott Oatsvall's timely, prophetic and times and seasons-clarifying book, *Seed Wars*

Endorsements

gives you a behind-the-veil look into the reason behind this present moment of cultural crisis: the seed of the serpent continues to make war against God's seed, His people. History, theology, prophecy, spiritual warfare and current events collide in this timely book, giving you the upper-hand advantage in exercising spiritual dominion over the forces of darkness. Portals are opened, and mass deception is clearly invading the planet. It's time for the victorious Ekklesia to arise and boldly proclaim Truth and witness a tidal wave of deliverance bring liberation to the masses under the influence of these demonic seeds.

Larry Sparks, M.Div.
LM Sparks Ministries
Publisher, Destiny Image
Author of *Pentecostal Fire*

Jesus said, "Just as it was in the days of Noah, so also will it be in the days of the Son of Man." (Luke 17:26). At the time of Noah, evil was so rampant and all-consuming among the inhabitants of the earth that God chose to destroy the entire population and start over with Noah and his family. We cannot afford to misunderstand what Jesus was saying about this as it applies to our generation and bury our heads in the sand. The signs of the fallen ones who lived prior to the flood have returned, but few believers realize it or even know what it means.

Dr. Greg Hood and Dr. Scott Oatsvall have worked together to produce a manuscript called *Seed Wars*, in which they explain and expound upon many biblical texts from the book of Genesis and elsewhere in scripture that reveal the meaning and long-term plans behind many of the demonic cultural manifestations we are experiencing today. The body of Christ is largely unaware of the level of demonic spiritual activity happening or how to respond to it properly. In this book, you will find many insights and directives that will aid you in overcoming the "spirit of the age," and I suggest you read it thoughtfully and prayerfully.

Joan Hunter, Evangelist/Author
Host of *Miracles Happen* TV show
President of 4WBN.TV

If there was ever a Kairos moment for a book to be revealed to the earth and the church, the time is now. From ancient times to the present, Dr. Greg Hood and Dr. Scott Oatsvall take us behind the scenes of the natural and into the supernatural to uncover the activities of the kingdom of darkness in the realm of the spirit. The book *Seed Wars* is a critical spiritual manual for the end-time church!

Isaac Pitre
Founder, Christ Nations Church
2Kings Global Network
Isaacpitre.org

Dr. Hood and Dr. Oatsvall have aligned their talents, training, and passions to produce the book, *Seed Wars*. The authors invite the reader to look beyond the seen realm or the temporal realm and to discover the reality of the unseen realm. From days of antiquity, throughout pagan nations, and in the Hebrew culture, people groups believed in and interacted with beings known to them as gods. At the dawn of the modern era, people became convinced that human reason and scientific discoveries could bring humanity to an epoch of enlightenment and utopia. Mankind, in effect, shifted his

Endorsements

focus away from the unseen. Two world wars, the discovery of nuclear weapons, and many other tragic human sufferings led to disillusionment and introduced the era of post-modernism, which reflected a general distrust of grand theories and ideologies of modernity. As in days of old, people began again to seek knowledge and experiences that had origins beyond the earthly dimensions. New age, mysticism, occultism, Harry Potter, and even old-world paganism have emerged as people have shifted their focus back to the unseen. The church must be present to answer questions that the populace is asking. The ekklesia must understand the unseen realm and bring clarity as to who the deities are, what roles they have played, and the supremacy of the God of Scriptures. Dr. Hood and Dr. Oatsvall have hearts to tell the eternal story of the seed war battle, and they have the knowledge to bring clarity about what has happened and is happening in the other-worldly dimensions. They present the truth concerning the giants and demons in the Bible. They introduce topics that will stir the reader to go further into the biblical narrative of seed wars. This book is a must-read!

Dr. Patti Amsden
Founder of East Gate Reformation Training Institute and Patti Amsden Ministries.
Dr. Amsden has authored ten books and travels extensively throughout the States and other nations teaching God's Words and raising up a generation of reformers.
www.pattiamsden.org

The authors have teamed up to bring the Body of Christ, a well-researched, well-written, and well-timed book.

In this contemporary season of seismic shaking in the world and in the Church, this prophetic book will inform, strengthen, and steer the followers of King Jesus. Whether we can fully define it or not, we know intuitively that we are called to a new level of spiritual warfare in this hour. We are becoming increasingly aware that spiritual warfare is the root of the cultural and political wars of our day!

The authors have unveiled the high-level historical and contemporary evil entities that confront us, mystify us, and seek to disrupt the plans and purposes of the Creator—Redeemer, Lord God of the Bible.

History is clearly seen in the light of the seed wars, which are first referred to in Genesis 3:15. Bible scholars refer to this verse as the protoevangelium. The message is the Good News, i.e., the Gospel of the victory of the Seed of the woman over the seed of the Serpent. The Seed of the Woman crushes the seed of the Serpent in his head, and simultaneously, the Seed of the Serpent bruises the heel of the Seed of the Woman. This happens at Calvary.

I very much appreciate how the authors present not only the real challenges we face from evil entities but also document that we are not defined by these evil giants. We are defined by the horizon of hope because of Christ's victory over evil powers through His death and resurrection! Goliaths lose; Davids win!

We, the Ekklesia Church, were launched by the breath of the Son of God on Resurrection night, and by the Father and Son teaming up to send us the Holy Spirit at Pentecost!

You and I are launched to advance and implement the agenda of the Kingdom of God in history on earth. Christ's return will be the culmination of this historic process!

Dr. Jim Hodges
Founder and President of the Federation of Ministers and Churches International

Endorsements

Dr. Greg Hood and Dr. Scott Oatsvall have lifted the veil off Holy Scripture and ancient credible sources to reveal the truth that greatly impacts our present world! Written with careful attention to the links between historical biblical statements about giants, the Nephilim, Artificial Intelligence, and as the "seed" of Yahweh, our present spiritual warfare. It is an absolutely amazing book: thorough, honest, scholarly, clear and totally biblical!

Here is the volume to introduce the reader to these subjects in an understandable way. The book shares fearful present struggles with our sure victory through faith in Christ!

Dr. Ron Phillips, D. Min
Pastor Emeritus Abba's House, Chattanooga, TN
Fresh Oil Ministries

Seed Wars is a spiritual and scientific exposé on the mystery of iniquity. It offers both biblical and historical insights into the operations of evil on earth. This book reveals how the spirits of darkness came from heaven to earth to influence and control civilizations. The truths presented in this book also inspire the people of the Kingdom of God to become warriors, reclaiming territories in heaven, on earth, and in the souls of men for the Lord Jesus Christ!

Tony Kemp
President of ACTS GROUP

Apostle Greg Hood and Dr. Scott Oatsvall present an intriguing exploration in *Seed Wars* to help us understand the serpent's end-time war against humanity. This war has been ongoing since the beginning of time, throughout history, and is still evident in our times. Many believers have dismissed the enemy's Nephilim agenda as a mere conspiracy, but *Seed Wars* reveals the antichrist agenda and urges us to take heed of the words in Isaiah 8:12: "You are not to say it is a conspiracy! Regarding all these people call a conspiracy, you are not to fear what they fear or dread it." *Seed Wars* serve as a clarion call to all believers to upgrade our knowledge and understand the present warfare so that these ancient demonic technologies would not deceive us. It's time to take down the giants of our day!

Prophet Myles Kilby
East Gate Church, Myles Kilby Intl., Brunswick, GA

There is a war going on! According to Drs. Greg Hood and Scott Oatsvall, this war is as old as creation and as up-to-date as the morning news. Drawing from biblical and extra-biblical texts, and scholarly research, these authors expose the enemy's plans to corrupt the "Good Seed." Their urgent message is a wake-up call, challenging the status quo and upsetting the apple cart of traditional thinking. Some of us need to open our eyes and realize that the enemy wants us to believe that all is lost and there is no hope for victory. But we must remember no matter what the world, the flesh and the devil attempt to do: "You are of God, little children, and have overcome them because He who is in you is greater than he who is in the world" (1 John 4:4).

I highly recommend reading this book and buying one for a friend without hesitation—you won't be disappointed.

Dr. J. Tod Zeiger
todzeigerministries.com, San Antonio, Texas

Endorsements

Dr. Greg Hood and Dr. Scott Oatsvall will challenge your understanding of today's war against evil forces in their book *Seed Wars*! The revelation of the battle between good and evil stirs the reader to see beyond traditional bible stories about giants in the land. The war is real! Believers must guard against deception and maintain strong faith in the Lord as we battle for the righteous Seed to overcome evil. God's Seed planted in the hearts of His human creation is more powerful than Satan's Seed! God's Seed promises to win the war against Satan's Seed!

Barbara Wentroble
President: International Breakthrough Ministries (IBM)
Speaker; Author

Seed Wars is a groundbreaking exploration of one of the most profound and complex cosmic conflicts recorded in ancient scriptures. This compelling work touches the eternal struggle between the seeds of God and the seeds of Satan, illuminating the ancient battle that has shaped human history since the dawn of time. This book is an essential read for anyone seeking to understand the spiritual dimensions of our world and the looming challenges we face. It equips believers with the knowledge and faith to stand firm against the great deception and embrace God's promises with confidence. *Seed Wars* is a testament to the enduring power of faith and the ultimate victory of divine truth over the forces of darkness.

Dr. Scott Reece
River City Church, Quad Cities
National Director at Kingdom Life Network

Finally, a book has come to give a plausible scriptural basis that many of us have suspected for decades. Dr. Greg Hood and his colleague Dr. Scott Oatsvall have masterfully given us a look into the unseen realm through the eyes of end-time events. Every serious intercessor and serious bible student will want to read and devour this writing. You will pray with more effectiveness, greater confidence and less shadow sparring with flesh and blood targets after reading this book.

You will no longer just scan Genesis 6, but you will look at it totally differently. The book you have in your hand will help take away mysticism and give you a more solid view of the final battle of the cosmos. You will also have more of a clear view as to the motive of the dark entities making their move in the last days. You will not come away from reading this piece with fear, but on the contrary, you will be encouraged to set your affection on the light of the Lord Jesus Christ.

I recommend this book to all who want to take a deeper dive into the Kingdom of God versus the Kingdoms of this World. It is well-written and not complicated to grasp. Thank you to Greg and Scott for giving us a masterpiece, and I am sure there is more to follow from these two writers.

Apostle Kerry Kirkwood
Senior Leader, Trinity Fellowship, Tyler, TX
Apostolic leader of Revive Leadership Network

In reading the manuscript for this book by my friend Greg Hood and Scott Oatsvall, I was very intrigued at how the book is preparing the Ekklesia for a future war against the seed of the serpent. Over the past year, Holy Spirit has sent me and my team on a journey to overthrow the principality, Pan. I had

Endorsements

never heard of Pan until October of 2023. I then discovered that Pan's temple and caves were where Yeshua took his disciples to Caesarea Philippi. He said to his followers, "Upon this Rock, I will build My Ekklesia." (Matthew 16:18). We also learned that Pan is the promoter of homosexuality, lesbianism, bestiality, child sacrifice, and many other despicable acts of darkness. By the end of 2024, we will have gone to 22 cities in Florida and Washington D.C. using Isaiah 22:15–22 as our weapon to dethrone this demon-god. My point in telling you about our assignment is to encourage you to think beyond the conventional boundaries of religion while reading *Seed Wars*. I believe that Yahweh is bringing together an Ekklesia for a final confrontation between the offspring of the serpent and the offspring of righteousness. Take the keys of the kingdom and forbid on earth what is forbidden in heaven and loose on earth what has been loosed in heaven. (Matthew 18:19) I'm looking forward to getting my copy of this book and gleaning strategy for the future.

Apostle Ken Malone
Kingdom Gate Worship Center
Satellite Beach, Florida

We've always been told that there are certain topics that you just do not bring up in conversation. We were given that advice regarding religion and politics. But now we, the Ekklesia, are seriously talking about these topics. We were also told about that. But there is one that still remains "taboo." It's the topic of the Nephilim. People give me that look whenever I've brought it up in conversation. They say that's just a conspiracy. They declare that it's not found in the biblical record. On the whole, it is disregarded as frivolous and unimportant.

However, in the book *Seed Wars* by Dr. Greg Hood and Dr. Scott Oatsvall, they take on this topic with full force. We must ask the Holy Spirit to give us revelation, for it forms much of the background views that we see being expressed by the Spirit-led writers of the biblical narrative that were hidden in extra-biblical materials. When I first heard them teach on this, I felt my brain needed to be unscrambled. The transformative power of this Holy Spirit's revelation has indeed unscrambled my thoughts, and these two friends speak a well-needed truth into the warfare that we need to be a part of in this hour as the Ekklesia.

Dr. Tom Schlueter
Texas Apostolic Prayer Network

Seed Wars is a captivating and thought-provoking exploration of one of the Bible's most mysterious passages. Dr. Greg Hood and Dr. Scott Oatsvall skillfully unravel the Nephilim's complexities, drawing on a rich tapestry of biblical and extra-biblical texts.

Their thorough research and insightful analysis provide a fresh perspective on Genesis 6:1–4.

The mixing of fallen angels with the daughters of men produces a race of trans-humans who challenge the very existence of our society as we know it. The authors walk through these ancient biblical narratives in new and meaningful ways, giving answers and perspective to modern-day Spiritual activity, warfare and phenomena.

What sets this book apart is its ability to bridge the past and present, revealing how the mixed seeds of the past are still amongst us today. They must be recognized, overcome and conquered by the sons and daughters of God in this generation.

Seed Wars is a must-read for anyone interested in deepening their understanding of the last days.

Matthew 24:37 says, "But as the days of Noah were, so shall also the coming of the Son of man. "We are in those days.

I wholeheartedly endorse *Seed Wars* as an essential resource for anyone eager to uncover the truths hidden in scripture and engage with these last days' profound questions.

Mary Wildish
Senior Pastor Trumpet Call Ministries.
Montego Bay, Jamaica.

Dr. Hood and Dr. Oatsvall have given us a clear vocabulary for understanding the origin and continuation of the great warfare between the two kingdoms. I applaud them for the clear interpretation of this spiritual conflict. They have defined what many of us have known in our spirit about spiritual warfare. *Seed Wars* is a must-read and a great contribution to the Kingdom of God!

Dr. Dwain Miller
Pastor, The Edge Church
Cabot AR

Jesus said in Matthew 24:37, "But as the days of Noah were, so shall also the coming of the Son of man be." This saying has been a mystery to church leaders and scholars for ages. It has not been until recent times that those with prophetic insight within the Ekklesia have come to understand the true meaning of this verse. Dr. Greg Hood & Dr. Scott have done a wonderful job in *Seed Wars: Unveiling the Agenda of the Nephilim Giants*, pulling the mask off of thousands of years old Satanic scheme to corrupt mankind that still exists in our day and hour. With the emergence of globalism, advanced biotechnology, AI, and strange genetics, this wicked Nephilim agenda presents a greater challenge than ever to the God-given destiny of mankind. Reading this book will help you understand the biblical, historical, and present-day development of the Nephilim defilement and how to avoid being deceived by the enemy. This is a power-packed book of revelation, truth, research, and divine insight.

Demontae Edmonds
President, Destiny 4 the Nations Inc.
Overseer, The Fathers House Ministry Network
Author of *The Supernatural Dimension of Dreams and Discerning of Spirits: 7 Dimensions of Revelation*

Not many ministers address Genesis 6:1–4 because defining the use of our current tools is controversial and challenging. While the average Christian asks the tough questions about this text, all they get in return is half-baked truths, if anything at all.

As a Kingdom University student, we've been taught a few questions to ask as we read the Bible, if we are to address the text in its most profound way. Who was the author? Who was the author writing to? What did it mean to them? What does it now mean to me?

Dr. Greg Hood and Dr. Scott Oatsvall set the table for a great discussion. It's a thought-provoking, logical, and very informative look into our history reimagined. This is what

Endorsements

makes it challenging. The narrative resets your thinking. Following the four questions, we find our answers. What then are the questions? Who were the sons of God? Who are the daughters of man? Who were the Nephilim? And what was their role in biblical history?"

Following the traditions of men, we don't find the answers to these questions. What if the history concerning Greek gods we thought was all fake is real? The meaning of the text of Genesis 6:1–4 is revealed in *Seed Wars*. The answers are here! Open your mind and relearn our history by reading.

We need these answers if we're going to put this passage in perspective and learn the whole of what happened then and now. This book is a must-read. It may very well be the most educational piece regarding the narrative of Genesis 6:1–4. I challenge all readers to glean what you can.

Howard Keith Long
Sergeant Major, U. S. Marine Corps (Retired)
COO at Kingdom University
House Church Pastor at Kingdom Life Ekklesia, Franklin, TN

Dr. Greg Hood and Dr. Scott Oatsvall are two men I greatly respect. I have known and ministered alongside them for several years. When they told me the title of the book they were writing was *Seed Wars*, it caught my attention. In my experience, many believers do not understand fundamental and foundational truths.

Seed Wars is not just a book; it's a revelation. It introduces a profound idea that has the power to shift your perspective of God's eternal purpose. The truths it presents and other kingdom revelations will open your eyes to what God is doing and will do in the days ahead, providing a new and enlightened understanding.

I encourage the reader to hear and consider the truths presented in *Seed Wars*. With this revelation, you will have greater insight into what God did in the past and why He did it. This will help you align yourself with God's eternal purpose as you live your life for him today!

God bless you in your journey to fulfill your part of God's eternal purpose.

Prophet Mitch Clay
Proclamation Ministries
Kingdom Life Network Apostolic Council Member

If there was ever a book that has met its time, it is *Seed Wars*. This book is not for the casual reader but for those who want to go beyond the surface of Scripture to mine out the truths for today. *Seed Wars* gives answers to what we are now experiencing daily. It answers questions that have left people shaking their heads and asking, "What in the world is happening." This book connects the dots to explain the war that has, for millennia, been taking place between two kingdoms and the increased escalation of that war today, where the powers of darkness have unashamedly dropped all smokescreens and are blatantly in the face of believers around the world. *Seed Wars* will leave you asking for more!

Donna Wise
Apostolic Leader of Impact Church International
Co-Founder and CEO of Genesis…A New Beginning Mental Health, Co-Founder of TMS of the Carolinas

Endorsements

I've spent years gleaming books and audios that involved the Nephilim agenda. None, in my opinion, are as concise and as well put together as *Seed Wars*. Greg and Scott offer numerous resources that help paint a clear picture of the true driving force behind what's at stake in our Nation and in the World. We can no longer suppress the truth about what's behind this wicked activity. Our response should be to rise above these covert activities and wield our Sword to fight for our children to preserve a righteous seed for generations. *Seed Wars* is an eye-opener for modern-day giant killers. We need not be afraid but rather gleam from the heroes of Faith as we continue to work with The King for Divine strategies. Thank you both for your bold stand for Truth. United We Stand!

Gloria D. Steele
RiverGate NEI Ministries
Regional Apostolic Leeder at Kingdom Life Network

Reading books by Greg Hood always sparks a spiritual hunger within me, urging me to delve deeper and learn more about the Kingdom. What Dr. Greg and Dr. Scott have done in their book, *Seed Wars*, had the same effect on me as Greg's previous work, *Gospel of the Kingdom*. It left me yearning for more, eager to continue reading and gain further revelation. Once you pick it up, you won't want to put it down. The warriors they write about embody the essence of the good seeds! It's time for the warriors to rise and be prepared to fight the good fight. As God's word teaches us, people perish for their lack of knowledge. This book is a must-read. The urgency of its message compels us to READ IT NOW! Let's Go!

Kraig Bougher, Founder of Ignite Christian Business

Seed Wars is an essential read for anyone seeking to delve deeper into the cosmic battle between good and evil, particularly in the historical context of the Nephilim story in the Bible.

Dr. Greg Hood and Dr. Scott Oatsvall present a compelling exploration of the Nephilim and the surrounding biblical lore. They skillfully connect ancient texts to modern theological interpretations, providing a framework for understanding the implications of Genesis 6:1–4. Their argument for the significance of extra-biblical texts is well-articulated, making a strong case for their inclusion in the study of biblical history.

The book's language is accessible yet scholarly, appealing to both lay readers and academics interested in biblical studies. Seed Wars successfully integrates cultural and historical contexts, consequently enriching the narrative and making it a valuable resource for those seeking to understand the complexities of the biblical account of the Nephilim.

Seed Wars is an insightful contribution to the discourse surrounding biblical texts on the Nephilim. It challenges readers to exercise critical thinking and further explore the complexities of biblical theology.

Pastor Ted Pangilinan, Senior Pastor and Founder, Church One Christian Community, Australia

Seed Wars

<u>Unraveling the Hidden History of</u>

<u>the Nephilim and Modern Deception</u>

Dr. Greg Hood, Ph.D., Th.D.

Dr. Scott Oatsvall, Ph.D.

Copyright

Seed Wars

Unraveling the Hidden History of the Nephilim and Modern Deception

Copyright © 2024 by Greg Hood

Published by Ekklesia Publishing. All rights reserved.

This book is protected by the copyright laws of the United States of America. This book may not be copied or reprinted for commercial gain or profit. The use of short quotations or occasional page copying for personal or group study is encouraged. Permission will be granted upon request from Ekklesia Publishing. Unless otherwise stated, all biblical quotations are taken from the NASB. All rights reserved. Any emphasis added to Scripture quotations is the author's own.

Scripture quotations marked NASB are taken from the New American Standard Bible, © 1960, 1962, 1963, 1968, 1971, 1972, 1973, 1975, 1977, 1995 by the Lockman Foundation. Used by permission.

Editing by Jim Bryson (JamesLBryson@gmail.com)

Graphics by David Munoz (davidmunoznvtn@gmail.com)

Contents

Foreword 1
Introduction 5
<u>Part I</u> Biblical and Extra-Biblical 7
   1. The Importance of Extra-Biblical Text ... 9
   2. The Origins of The Seed Wars 15
   3. The Good Seeds 23
   4. The Evil Seeds 29
   5. Seeds of Deception 37
   6. The Digital Seeds 45
   7. Giants of Yore 51
   8. Clash of the Titans 55
   9. The Mixing of Seeds 61
   10. The Final Seed 65
<u>Part II</u> Further Evidence 71
   11. Where Have All the Bones Gone? 73
   12. The Giants of North America 79
   13. The Elongated Skulls Of Peru 97
About the Authors 107

Dedication

From Dr. Greg Hood

I dedicate this work to the remnant Ekklesia (Church) and all those who hunger for wisdom and revelation on this topic. You are the forerunners, leading the way as the tip of the spear. Keep pressing on! Giants are falling! Yeshua wins!

From Dr. Scott Oatsvall

I dedicate this work to the blessed and the elect that the ancient writers called the "remote generation to come." We ARE that generation that will be living in the days of tribulation. We are the modern-day giant slayers. Get your slingshots ready!

Finally, I would like to dedicate this book to our beloved son Joseph Oatsvall, who went to be with the Lord Jesus Christ this year. Although our loss crushes us, we know our future with our son will be longer than our past. We love you JOJO!

Acknowledgments

From Dr. Greg Hood

First and foremost, I want to thank my bride, Joan Sobrepeña Hood, who has survived hours upon hours of me relaying my research and sermons on this topic. No one should have to bear such. LOL! I am very grateful to you, and I love you very much, Sinta Ko. You are my motivation!

I want to thank Dr. Scott Oatsvall for co-writing this work with me. I could not have done it without you, my friend. Your scientific knowledge and understanding of the supernatural realm are priceless. I am thankful for our partnership in getting this message out to all who would receive it.

A very Special thank you to L.A. Marzulli, whose Foreword for this new work is a testament to his unparalleled influence in this sphere of influence. His tireless commitment, extensive research, and prolific book writing and movie-making on this topic far exceed mine. Sir, your dedication to your assignment has significantly advanced the Ekklesia's understanding of the supernatural. Your unique contributions have set a high standard that I aspire to. Sometimes I find myself saying, "When I grow up, I want to be like L.A."

Thank you to all my friends and colleagues who endorsed this book. Your theological insights and occasional corrections have been invaluable in shaping this work. Your contributions have added depth and clarity to this project, and I am eternally grateful for your impact on my life.

A huge thank you to Jim Bryson! Sir, you are a Shogun among editors! (Driving a Honda Ridgeline truck has its perks.) You will probably dream about Nephilim for the next six months. (But wait, there is another book in the making!) Thank you for staying in the trenches of this work to get it done. And I also want to give a big shoutout to Jacqueline Bryson. Thank you for all that you do behind the scenes. We all know Jim couldn't be the gentleman that he is without you.

A big thank you to Keith Long, Kathleen Bullock, and Carrol McDonnell for your meticulous proofreading. Your attention to detail and dedication to catching all my misspellings and grammatical mistakes have significantly improved the quality of this book.

Lastly, I want to express my heartfelt thanks to all of our Kingdom Life Ekklesia family, facility, pastors, and staff. Your unwavering support and the 'pulling' you often do to push me to dig deeper into research and the study of this topic have been invaluable. We are on this incredible, life-changing journey together, and I am grateful to each of you. KINGDOM COME!!

From Dr. Scott Oatsvall

I want to begin by expressing my deepest gratitude to my wife and best friend, Gwen Oatsvall, and to our wonderful children. Their unwavering support and patience during the years of my research have been a true blessing. I am incredibly fortunate to have such a loving family, and I am profoundly thankful for their sacrifices.

I also wish to acknowledge the pioneering scholars I consider mentors and who have guided my research: Dr. Chuck

Acknowledgments

Missler, Dr. Michael Heiser, and Rob Skiba. Your foundational work continues to resonate and inspire many.

A special thanks goes to L.A. Marzulli for writing the foreword for this work. His profound influence and relentless dedication to this field through extensive research, writing, and filmmaking have set a remarkable standard. I aspire to emulate his exceptional commitment and contributions to understanding the ancient world and unseen realms.

Lastly, I am grateful to my friend and brother, Dr. Greg Hood, for partnering with me on this most important project. We are on this battlefield together to expose the Nephilim agenda and the spiritual forces of darkness.

Foreword

by L.A. Marzulli

And I will put enmity (open hostility) Between you and the woman, And between your seed (offspring) and her Seed; He shall [fatally] bruise your head, And you shall [only] bruise His heel.

Genesis 3:15 (Amplified Bible)

I believe Genesis 3:15 is the gateway to the biblical prophetic narrative. Understanding this passage is not just helpful but a crucial element to grasping the seed war and its profound implications. This book you hold is an excellent means to broach the subject that most churches won't touch. Sadly, the people in the pews remain ignorant of the great cosmic war raging all around us.

If you want to keep people in the dark spiritually and supernaturally, never explain the seed war that we read about in Genesis 3:15. Thus, the people remain ignorant and have no clue as to the ongoing war that has been raging, not only in the heavenly realm but also here on earth.

These are the people that the prophet Hosea wrote about:

> My people are destroyed for lack of knowledge.
> Since you have rejected knowledge,
> I also will reject you from being My priest.

> Since you have forgotten the Law of your God,
> I also will forget your children.
>
> Hosea 4:6

Jesus further warns us that it will be like Noah's days when the Son of Man returns.

> But as the days of Noah were, so shall also the coming of the Son of man be.
>
> Matthew 24:37

Think about it: out of all the scriptures in the TANAKH that Jesus could reference, He points to Genesis 6. Dr. Greg Hood and Dr. Scott Oatsvall have illuminated this passage with great erudition, and while it might stretch some of us out of our comfort zones, their exegesis is spot on.

We are living in unprecedented times. Everything that Jesus warned us about—wars and rumors of wars, famines, pestilence, earthquakes in diverse places and troublesome times—is firing in concert.

Jesus said,

> Watch out for doomsday deceivers. Many leaders are going to show up with forged identities, claiming, "I am Christ, the Messiah." They will deceive a lot of people. When reports come in of wars and rumored wars, keep your head and don't panic. This is routine history; this is no sign of the end. Nation will fight nation and ruler fight ruler, over and over. Famines and earthquakes will occur in various places. This is nothing compared to what is coming.
>
> Matthew 24:6–8 (The Message Bible)

Foreword

Students of the Bible who study prophecy should be amazed to find themselves living in a time when many of these ancient prophetic texts will be fulfilled.

A few years ago, I came up with a saying:

> What was written will come to pass; what was foretold is unfolding.

Dr. Greg Hood and Dr. Scott Oatsvall have delved into the prophetic passages and woven a tapestry of end-time events through careful study and exegesis.

I challenge you to read this book. I also urge you to consider buying a few copies to give to loved ones, especially pastors.

Folks, we are undeniably in the end times, and this excellent tome will help you understand and navigate the turbulent waters of these last days. The urgency of our current situation cannot be overstated. It's time to equip ourselves with the knowledge and understanding of the *Seed Wars*!

Dr. L. A. Marzulli
CEO–Spiral of Life,
Author/Filmmaker

Introduction

There is an unseen realm where the eternal struggle between the seeds of God and the seeds of Satan rages. This profound cosmic conflict has unfolded since the dawn of time. This is the story of the "Seed Wars," a titanic battle that revolves around the essence of creation and the attempt to defile the very thing God created in His own image.

At the heart of this epic confrontation lie the seeds of God and Satan, embodying the purest expressions of good and evil. From the heavenly realms to the deepest abyss, these divine and evil forces have clashed for supremacy over the fabric of existence itself.

As this battle for the human soul continues, we find ourselves drawn back to the age of Genesis 6, where an extraordinary narrative emerges.

The ancient scriptures tell of fallen angels descending to Earth in physical form and committing an illegal act against God, seeking to create a hybrid race of humans known as the Nephilim. These were the offspring of fallen angels and human women, bridging the gap between the celestial and the earthly.

Yet, amidst the celestial and earthly intermingling, a sinister plot emerged from the shadows. The enemies of humanity, driven by malice and envy, sought to defile the purity of the human genome. Their vile machinations aimed to corrupt the very seed of mankind, defiling God's creations.

Let's not be fooled into believing that the Nephilim were only present in the ancient world. Their influence persists today, with their agenda continuing to shape our world. They are the powerful entities behind global governance, having penetrated every facet of our lives. This resurgence, combined with emerging threats such as artificial intelligence (AI), has led to an unprecedented confluence of challenges.

In our book, *Seed Wars*, we will expose the Nephilim agenda and prepare God's children for the ultimate showdown—an apocalyptic clash between the forces of light, darkness, and the great deception.

Prepare to embark on a journey through the annals of time, where the cosmic battle between the seeds of God and the seeds of Satan unfolds before your very eyes. In *Seed Wars*, ancient prophecies shall be fulfilled, heroes will rise, and the future of the Ekklesia will be established!

Part I
Biblical and Extra-Biblical

1

The Importance of Extra-Biblical Text

The Bible is the world's most widely read and studied religious text. However, several extra-biblical texts provide additional information on biblical events and characters. These texts include the Book of Enoch, the Book of Giants, the Book of Jasher, the Book of Jubilees, and others. These texts are essential in understanding Genesis 6:1–4, which has been debated and analyzed for centuries.

Genesis 6:1–4 reads:

> When men began to multiply on the face of the land and daughters were born to them, the sons of God saw that the daughters of man were attractive. And they took as their wives any they chose. Then the Lord said, 'My Spirit shall not abide in man forever, for he is flesh: his days shall be 120 years.' The Nephilim were on the earth in those days, and also afterward, when the sons of God came into the daughters of man, they bore children to them. These were the mighty men who were of old, the men of renown.

This passage has raised many questions over the years. Who were the "sons of God"? Who were the "daughters of man"? Who were the Nephilim? And what was their role in biblical history? These questions have led scholars and theologians to turn to extra-biblical texts for answers.

So why are these extra-biblical texts important in understanding Genesis 6:1–4? For one, they provide additional information on the characters and events mentioned in the passage. These texts also help shed light on the cultural and religious context in which the Bible was written. The ancient texts provide insight into the beliefs and practices of the people who wrote and read them. For example, the Book of Enoch depicts a world where angels and humans interacted, and forbidden knowledge was pursued and sought after. The Book of Giants reveals a world in which giants were feared and revered and in which divine beings played a role in human affairs.

The Book of Enoch

The Book of Enoch is a collection of writings attributed to Enoch, a figure from the Old Testament. It was a significant part of the culture in Jesus' day, the second temple period. Jesus and several New Testament writers either quoted or referred to the Book of Enoch in their writings. It records some pretty wild and crazy things. Enoch was said to have been taken up to heaven by God. The book provides a detailed account of the fallen angels who took human wives and fathered the Nephilim, the giants mentioned in Genesis. According to the scribe of Enoch, these angels were led by a Watcher named Azazel, who taught them forbidden knowledge and how to make weapons. The Nephilim were known for their great strength and violence. The Book of Enoch also describes the fallen angels' punishment and the fate of the Nephilim. This book is vital to Believers as it offers a more detailed account of the fallen angels and their role in human history, providing a glimpse into the beliefs and practices of ancient peoples. Also, the Book of Enoch challenges readers to think critically about the biblical text and its interpretation. We encourage you to get a copy of the Book of Enoch, especially 1 Enoch, and read it with an open mind and heart, closely observing similarities to passages you have read in the New Testament.

The Book of Giants

The Book of Giants is a fragmentary text found among the Dead Sea Scrolls in the caves of Qumran. It tells the story of the Nephilim from the perspective of their offspring, describing them as monstrous beings who were both feared and worshiped by ancient peoples. For believers, the Book of Giants is an important study tool. It provides additional information about the Nephilim and their influence on ancient societies. The book gives us insight into the forbidden knowledge that the fallen angels taught humanity, such as astrology, divination, the art of war, and—are you ready for this?—women's cosmetics. It also helps us understand the cultural and religious context in which the Bible was written, and it deepens our understanding of historical biblical theology.

In summary, the Book of Giants is an important extra-biblical text because it sheds much light on the Nephilim and their influence upon those who lived in their day. It is a valuable resource offering an understanding of the forbidden knowledge that the fallen angels imparted to humanity.

The Book of Jasher

The Book of Jasher is a lesser-known text, but it is still important for understanding Genesis 6:1–4. It is a historical chronicle covering the period from Adam to Joshua's conquest of Canaan. The Book of Jasher contains additional details on the Nephilim and their offspring and provides more information on the fallen angels who fathered them. For example, the book describes how the Nephilim became corrupt and evil, leading to their destruction in the Flood.

The Book of Jasher is also a critical extra-biblical text for Believers because it offers a much broader historical context for the events described in Genesis 6:1–4. This once lost asset helps readers understand the characters and events mentioned in the Bible and can deepen their understanding of biblical theology.

Extra-Biblical Texts

These extra-biblical texts are noteworthy because of the additional information on the characters and events mentioned in Genesis 6:1–4. Let's review. We have seen that the Book of Enoch, for example, provides a more detailed account of the fallen angels and their role in human history. The Book of Giants offers more information on the Nephilim and their impact on ancient societies. The Book of Jasher provides a broader historical context for the events described in Genesis 6:1–4.

Moreover, these texts help to illuminate the cultural and religious context in which the Bible was written. They provide a glimpse into the beliefs and practices of the ancient peoples who wrote and read these texts. The Book of Enoch depicts a world where angels and humans interacted, and forbidden knowledge was sought after and highly valued. The Book of Giants reveals a world in which giants were feared and revered and in which divine beings played a role in human affairs.

These extra-biblical texts can help to deepen our understanding of the Bible as a whole. They provide a richer and more complicated picture of biblical history and theology.

They also challenge us to think critically about the biblical text and its interpretation. By exploring these texts, we are forced to grapple with difficult questions about God's nature, humanity's role in the world, and the relationship between the divine and the human, the seen and the unseen realms.

In conclusion, the Book of Enoch, the Book of Giants, and the Book of Jasher are important extra-biblical texts that provide beneficial information on Genesis 6:1–4 and biblical history in general. They help us understand the characters and events mentioned in the Bible, clarify the cultural and religious context in which the Bible was written, and deepen our understanding of biblical theology. These texts are essential readings for anyone interested in biblical studies and theology.

Their writings were not included in the Protestant Canon of scripture but are related to it somehow. These texts are important to believers as study tools alongside the Bible because they provide valuable insight into the cultural and historical context in which the Bible was written and offer additional information that can help us better understand the characters and events mentioned in the Word of God.

They are valuable study tools for Believers because they provide additional information on the characters and events mentioned in the Bible. Additionally, they help challenge us to think critically about the Bible and its interpretation. We should read the Bible and engage with these extra-biblical texts to deepen our understanding of biblical history and theology.

The Bible is the world's most widely read and studied manuscript, but it doesn't tell the full story. Genesis 6:1–4 is a passage debated and analyzed for centuries, and these extra-biblical texts are essential to understanding the whole story.

2

The Origins of The Seed Wars

...the sons of God saw that the daughters of mankind were beautiful; and they took wives for themselves, whomever they chose.

Genesis 6:2

Who are the "sons of God"?

There are three main views about the identity of the "sons of God" mentioned in Genesis 6:2. Let's explore the most popular views:

Sethite View

According to the Sethite view, the "sons of God" were godly men from Seth's family line, and the "daughters of men" were ungodly women from Cain's family line. When these godly men married the ungodly women, their offspring became wicked and gained notoriety for their evil deeds.

Arguments for this view emphasize that the Bible already focuses on the descendants of Cain and Seth, so there's no need to introduce external ideas. Some of Seth's descendants, like Enoch and Noah, were known for their righteousness.

Objections

Critics of this view point out that the terms "men" and "daughters" are used in a universal sense earlier in Genesis 6:1:

> Now it came about, when mankind began to multiply on the face of the land, and daughters were born to them,

This suggests a broader scope of humanity. Also, not all of Cain's descendants were necessarily evil. If Seth's men were godly, why did they continue marrying unbelieving women? And why would God destroy the entire world for something that has been happening throughout history (believers marrying unbelievers)?

Royalty View

The royalty view sees the "sons of God" as powerful kings or rulers who saw themselves as gods. These kings would take women from the common people to add to their harems, leading to famous and renowned offspring.

Arguments for this view are that some ancient texts show that some kings viewed themselves as divine. The children of kings and nobles were often notable figures. There are instances where the Hebrew word *elohim* is translated as "rulers" or "judges."

Objections to this view are that it's not necessarily wrong for kings to marry common women. The phrase "they took wives" doesn't imply polygamy or forced marriages, as it was a common idiom for marriage in Hebrew. Additionally, it might not be accurate to apply post-Flood ideas from ancient Near Eastern cultures to the pre-Flood world.

Fallen Angel View

According to the fallen angel view, the "sons of God" were heavenly beings (i.e. angels) who married human women and had offspring known as the Nephilim. Some early writers believed these offspring were demonic, but modern proponents argue that they were fully human.

Arguments for this view suggest that the phrases in the Hebrew Bible only refer to heavenly beings. Some New Testament passages also mention angels who sinned and were confined until judgment, linking them to the events of Noah's time.

Objections are that angels are spiritual beings, so the idea of them physically marrying humans is questioned. Jesus mentioned that angels don't marry in heaven. Also, there's no clear explanation for the post-flood Nephilim. Some critics doubt that fallen angels could manifest in physical form.

These views offer different perspectives on the "sons of God" in Genesis 6:2, but only one of them has actual scriptural support: that the sons of God were fallen angels.

The fallen angel view is supported by specific Bible scriptures and the Book of Enoch, making it the most comprehensive view of the three discussed. Here are the key reasons why:

Biblical References

Sons of God

The phrase "sons of God" is used frequently in the Bible.

<u>The Old Testament</u>

It occurs six times and always refers to angelic beings. In addition to Genesis 6:2 and 6:4, it is also found in other parts of the Bible.

> Now there was a day when the sons of God came to present themselves before the Lord, and Satan also came among them.
>
> Job 1:6
>
> Again, there was a day when the sons of God came to present themselves before the Lord, and Satan also came among them to present himself before the Lord.
>
> Job 2:1
>
> When the morning stars sang together
> And all the sons of God shouted for joy?
>
> Job 38:7

These scriptures refer to heavenly beings as "sons of God." This consistent usage indicates that the term typically denotes angels or divine beings.

The New Testament

We find additional support for the fallen angel view in the following scriptures.

> For Christ also suffered for sins once for all time, the just for the unjust, so that He might bring us to God, having been put to death in the flesh, but made alive in the spirit; in which He also went and made proclamation to the spirits in prison, who once were disobedient when the patience of God kept waiting in the days of Noah, during the construction of the ark, in which a few, that is, eight persons, were brought safely through the water.
>
> 1 Peter 3:18–20

> For if God did not spare angels when they sinned, but cast them into hell and committed them to pits of darkness, held for judgment; and did not spare the ancient world, but protected Noah, a preacher of

> righteousness, with seven others, when He brought a flood upon the world of the ungodly; and if He condemned the cities of Sodom and Gomorrah to destruction by reducing them to ashes, having made them an example of what is coming for the ungodly; and if He rescued righteous Lot, who was oppressed by the perverted conduct of unscrupulous people (for by what he saw and heard that righteous man, while living among them, felt his righteous soul tormented day after day by their lawless deeds), then the Lord knows how to rescue the godly from a trial, and to keep the unrighteous under punishment for the day of judgment, and especially those who indulge the flesh in its corrupt passion, and despise authority.
>
> Reckless, self-centered, they speak abusively of angelic majesties without trembling,
>
> 2 Peter 2:4–10

These references mention angels who sinned in the days of Noah and were subsequently bound in chains until judgment.

Jude 6 speaks of angels who left their proper abode and are kept in eternal chains.

> And angels who did not keep their own domain but abandoned their proper dwelling place, these He has kept in eternal restraints under darkness for the judgment of the great day,

These passages connect the "sons of God" in Genesis 6 with fallen angels.

Jude also makes reference to Enoch:

> It was also about these people that Enoch, in the seventh generation from Adam, prophesied, saying, "Behold, the Lord has come with many thousands of His holy

ones, to execute judgment upon all, and to convict all the ungodly of all their ungodly deeds which they have done in an ungodly way, and of all the harsh things which ungodly sinners have spoken against Him."

Jude 14–15

Jude quotes the Book of Enoch, an ancient Jewish apocryphal text, to support the idea that the "sons of God" were indeed heavenly beings who committed an illegal act against God and who sinned by marrying human women. While the Book of Enoch is not part of the modern-day canonical Bible, Jude's reference suggests that some early Christians considered it a valid source of information regarding the events of Genesis 6.

Clearly, Jude did.

The Book of Enoch

The Book of Enoch is an ancient Jewish work that elaborates on the events surrounding the "sons of God" and the Nephilim in Genesis 6. Although not included in the Bible, it was widely known and respected in Jewish and early Christian communities, including the early Church fathers.

The Book of Enoch expands on the fallen angel view, describing how heavenly beings, known as "Watchers," descended to Earth, lusted after human women, and took them as wives. These unions resulted in the birth of the Nephilim, who were described as powerful and wicked giants. The Book of Enoch provides additional details and context to the events in Genesis 6, supporting the idea that the "sons of God" were indeed fallen angels.

In conclusion, the fallen angel view aligns with various biblical references, such as passages in the Old and New Testaments linking the "sons of God" to fallen angels. Additionally, the Book of Enoch offers further insights into this perspective. While it is not the only interpretation of Genesis 6:2, it is the only view supported by scripture and provides a comprehensive and coherent understanding of the events described in the Genesis 6 account.

3

The Good Seeds

In the annals of ancient Hebrew history, an epic tapestry unfolds, woven with times of heroic deeds and valiant warriors for God who rose to face these super-hybrid humans. These champions of our faith, whom we will refer to as "good seeds," were skilled in battle and held an unwavering faith in their divine assignment to protect the very thing that God created in His likeness and image. Us! They stood firm against giants and tribes of giants, fearlessly defending their people and their lands.

These are our Heroes of the Bible—the mighty men and women of our faith. The good seeds of the Bible fought to preserve the human genome, and they had to battle against these giants and their tribes all throughout history.

So we embark on this supernatural journey that draws not only from the familiar scriptures but also lesser-known ancient texts like the Book of Enoch, Jasher, the Book of the Giants, and Jubilees, to unveil the remarkable stories of these good seeds- Abraham, Noah, and David's mighty men just to name a few.

Abraham—The Father of Many Nations

In Genesis 14, we encounter the remarkable story of Abraham, the patriarch chosen by God to become the father of many nations. When an alliance of kings took his nephew Lot captive, Abraham did not hesitate to muster his men and lead them into battle.

> Then they [the kings] took all the possessions of Sodom and Gomorrah and all their food supply, and departed. They also took Lot, Abram's nephew, and his possessions and departed, for he was living in Sodom.
>
> Then a survivor came and told Abram the Hebrew. Now he was residing by the oaks of Mamre the Amorite, brother of Eshcol and brother of Aner, and they were allies with Abram. When Abram heard that his relative had been taken captive, he led out his trained men, born in his house, numbering 318, and went in pursuit as far as Dan. Then he divided his forces against them by night, he and his servants, and defeated them, and pursued them as far as Hobah, which is north of Damascus. He brought back all the possessions, and also brought back his relative Lot with his possessions, and also the women, and the other people.
>
> Genesis 14: 11–16

Though outnumbered, Abraham (Abram) demonstrated his unwavering trust in Jehovah and fought off these tribes of giants, one after another.

The Book of Jasher further illuminates Abraham's valor, recounting his boldness in facing Nimrod, the great king and tyrant of his time. Refusing to bow to idolatry, Abraham fearlessly proclaimed the glory of the one true God, facing the wrath of Nimrod and his people. Despite the threats, Abraham remained steadfast, unyielding to the pressures of his age.

Noah—The Faithful Ark Builder

In the Book of Jubilees and other ancient texts, we find a detailed account of Noah's extraordinary obedience to God's command to build the Ark. Amidst a world ravaged by corruption and the tyranny of the Nephilim, Noah stood resolute, faithful to the divine plan.

The Book of Enoch sheds light on the fallen angels' role in the corruption of humanity. The blending and corruption of genetic species led to the rise of the Nephilim—giants who wreaked havoc upon the earth. In this dark era, Noah remained righteous, a beacon of hope amidst the chaos. His unwavering faith earned him the favor of Jehovah, preserving him and his family as the floodwaters cleansed the earth.

David's Mighty Men

The reign of King David was marked by his extraordinary band of mighty men, renowned for their courage and valor. In 2 Samuel 23, we encounter a list of some of these fearless warriors and their incredible feats as they fought the tribes of giants to cleanse the ancient world from this illegal act against God.

Here is a brief sample from verses 8–12.

> These are the names of the mighty men whom David had: Josheb-basshebeth, a Tahchemonite, chief of the captains; he was called Adino the Eznite because of eight hundred who were killed by him at one time. And after him was Eleazar the son of Dodo the Ahohite, one of the three mighty men with David when they defied the Philistines who were gathered there to battle and the men of Israel had withdrawn. He rose up and struck the Philistines until his hand was weary and it clung to the sword, and the Lord brought about a great victory that day; and the people returned after him only to plunder the dead.
>
> Now after him was Shammah the son of Agee, a Hararite. And the Philistines were gathered into an army

where there was a plot of land full of lentils, and the people fled from the Philistines. But he took his stand in the midst of the plot, defended it, and struck the Philistines; and the Lord brought about a great victory.

Another such hero was Benaiah, whose bravery extended beyond Israel's borders. From verses 20–23:

> Then Benaiah the son of Jehoiada, the son of a valiant man of Kabzeel, who had done great deeds, killed the two sons of Ariel of Moab. He also went down and killed a lion in the middle of a pit on a snowy day. And he killed an Egyptian, an impressive man. Now the Egyptian had a spear in his hand, but he went down to him with a club and snatched the spear from the Egyptian's hand and killed him with his own spear.
>
> These things Benaiah the son of Jehoiada did and had a name as well as the three mighty men. He was honored among the thirty, but he did not attain the reputation of the three. And David appointed him over his bodyguard.

In the Book of Jasher, we find an account of Benaiah's pursuit of a ferocious lion into a pit on a snowy day. With divine favor, he emerged victorious over this fierce adversary, illustrating that the good seeds' courage knew no bounds.

These mighty men's unwavering loyalty and unyielding commitment to God and their king exemplified the essence of the good seeds, standing resolute against giants and all odds.

The stories of the good seeds battling giants and tribes of giants in the Bible and the Books of Enoch, Jasher, the Book of the Giants, and Jubilees stand as timeless examples of courage, faith, and divine favor. These champions, like Abraham, Noah, and David's mighty men, remind us that when we align ourselves with righteousness and trust in

Jehovah, we can overcome any seemingly insurmountable challenge.

In every encounter with giants and tribes of giants, the good seeds recognized that they were instruments of God's will, and their triumphs were testimonies to His power and grace. Their unwavering faith in the Creator emboldened them to confront any foe that threatened the well-being of their people and the fulfillment of God's promises.

As we journey through the chapters of time, let us embrace the spirit of the good seeds and face our adversaries, knowing that with God's favor, we too can emerge triumphant. May the legacy of these ancient heroes inspire us to uphold righteousness, courage, and unwavering faith in the face of the giants that loom in our own lives. Just as the good seeds of old paved the way for victory, so too can we embrace our divine calling, knowing that we are not alone in our battles.

WE ARE THE MODERN-DAY
GIANT KILLERS!

4

The Evil Seeds

Have you ever wondered why God ordered his warriors to destroy certain tribes of the Old Testament, including the women, children and even the animals? It's because they were a genetically modified and defiled race of giants.

As we look at ancient Hebrew history, a dark and foreboding story continues to unfold, where tribes of giants, known as the Nephilim, Anakim, Rephaim, Canaanites, and Amorites, to name a few, loomed as formidable adversaries against God's people. Their origins, as we discussed in our introduction and also found in Genesis and in apocryphal texts like the Book of Enoch and the Book of Giants, trace back to the illegal act against God when unions between fallen angels and human women birthed offspring of immense strength and malevolence.

In this chapter, we will dive into some of these unsettling stories and understand the divine judgment that led to the command to destroy these tribes of hybrid beings.

As a review, the Nephilim of Genesis 6 were the offspring of fallen angels (known as the sons of God) and human women.

The haunting presence of the hybrid creatures cast a dark shadow over the pre-Flood world. As recounted in Genesis 6:1-4, these mighty giants became renowned for their power and violence, contributing to the moral decay that prompted God's judgment through the Great Flood.

In the Book of Enoch, the Watchers—a group of fallen angels—descended to earth and took human women as wives, resulting in the birth of the Nephilim. Their existence wreaked havoc upon humanity, teaching forbidden and sacred knowledge to humans and leading to widespread corruption. Their oppressive rule, as further elaborated in the Book of Giants, caused immense suffering and chaos.

The Anakim and Rephaim—Giants of the Promised Land

As God's chosen people journeyed towards the Promised Land, they encountered the fearsome tribes of giants known as the Anakim and Rephaim. The Anakim, descendants of Anak, were renowned for their towering stature and intimidating presence, as described in Numbers 13:28-33.

> Nevertheless, the people who live in the land are strong, and the cities are fortified and very large. And indeed, we saw the descendants of Anak there! Amalek is living in the land of the Negev, the Hittites, the Jebusites, and the Amorites are living in the hill country, and the Canaanites are living by the sea and by the side of the Jordan."

> Then Caleb quieted the people before Moses and said, "We should by all means go up and take possession of it, for we will certainly prevail over it." But the men who had gone up with him said, "We are not able to go up against the people, because they are too strong for us." So they brought a bad report of the land which they had spied out to the sons of Israel, saying, "The land through which we have gone to spy out is a land that devours its inhabitants; and all the people whom we saw in it are people of great stature. We also saw the Nephilim there

(the sons of Anak are part of the Nephilim); and we were like grasshoppers in our own sight, and so we were in their sight."

The existence of the Anakim in Canaan presented a significant test of faith for the Israelites, as they represented seemingly insurmountable obstacles standing between them and their promised inheritance.

The Rephaim, on the other hand, were mighty warriors and conquerors, often associated with legendary cities such as Bashan. Their formidable nature and battle domination instilled fear in neighboring regions' hearts. References to the Rephaim include:

> For only Og king of Bashan was left of the remnant of the Rephaim. Behold, his bed was a bed of iron; it is in Rabbah of the sons of Ammon. Its length was nine cubits, and its width four cubits by the usual cubit.
>
> Deuteronomy 3:11

> ...and the territory of Og king of Bashan, one of the remnant of Rephaim, who lived at Ashtaroth and at Edrei,
>
> Joshua 12:4

Divine Judgment and the Call for Destruction

Amidst the chaos and destruction wrought by these tribes of giants, divine judgment was meted out as a consequence of their wickedness and the corruption they brought upon the earth. God, in His sovereignty, decreed that their existence posed a grave danger to His people and His divine plan. Their perverse ways and rebellion against God's divine order demanded a severe response.

In the conquest of the Promised Land, God instructed the Israelite armies to execute a complete destruction of these tribes, including men, women, children, and even animals. The Book of Deuteronomy provides insight into God's reasoning, stating that the wicked practices of these nations, including idolatry, child sacrifice, and sexual immorality, defiled the land and invoked divine wrath.

> Do not say in your heart when the Lord your God has driven them away from you, "Because of my righteousness the Lord has brought me in to take possession of this land." Rather, it is because of the wickedness of these nations that the Lord is dispossessing them before you. It is not because of your righteousness or the uprightness of your heart that you are going in to take possession of their land, but it is because of the wickedness of these nations that the Lord your God is driving them out from before you, and in order to confirm the oath which the Lord swore to your fathers, to Abraham, Isaac, and Jacob.
>
> Deuteronomy 9:4–5

> When you enter the land which the Lord your God is giving you, you shall not learn to imitate the detestable things of those nations. There shall not be found among you anyone who makes his son or his daughter pass through the fire, one who uses divination, a soothsayer, one who interprets omens, or a sorcerer, or one who casts a spell, or a medium, or a spiritist, or one who consults the dead. For whoever does these things is detestable to the Lord; and because of these detestable things the Lord your God is going to drive them out before you.
>
> Deuteronomy 18:9–12

The tribes of giants, including the Nephilim, Anakim, Rephaim, Canaanites, and Amorites, were harbingers of chaos and destruction, causing immense suffering to God's people and the surrounding regions. Their existence epitomized the consequences of straying from divine order and indulging in wickedness and rebellion.

Divine judgment, though difficult to comprehend, was rooted in God's desire to protect His chosen people and preserve the integrity of the human genome.

The destruction commanded upon these tribes was a pivotal moment in history, marking God's unwavering commitment to righteousness and justice.

As we continue to look at the Seed Wars of God vs. Satan and we dive into these ancient accounts, may the references from the Bible, the Book of Enoch, and the Book of Giants deepen our understanding of these giants' malevolent influence. Let us glean wisdom and discernment from the principle that says, "condemnation without investigation will keep you in a state of ignorance!"

Categorizing the Evil Seeds

Ancient Hebrew history, as well as contemporary evidence, proves the existence of beings and entities that defy conventional understanding and challenge the essence of God's creation. So let's take a closer look and differentiate the bad seeds like the Nephilim, hybrid offspring, animal-human blending, and disembodied demonic spirits of giants, the Grey aliens and the Nordics. These entities have captivated the imaginations of many and have been a very controversial topic in the modern-day church. Let us take a high-resolution view into their unsettling presence and enigmatic alliances in the world of the bad seeds.

Hybrid Offspring of the Nephilim

Beyond the Nephilim, other accounts in apocryphal texts reveal unsettling descriptions of hybrid offspring resulting from unnatural unions between angels and various species. These hybrid beings blur the boundaries set by God, unsettling the natural order of life itself and engendering fearsome creatures of darkness. These were the tribes that we described earlier.

Next, we need to understand that these fallen angels were not only corrupting the human genome, but animals as well.

Ancient writings as well as oral traditions also describe dark experiments involving animal-human blending, where spiritual forces sought to manipulate the divine design and natural order of God. These unholy creations transgressed the sanctity of God's creation, yielding aberrations that challenge human understanding.

Demons

The next class of evil seed would be known as "demons"—the disembodied spirits of giants.

The malevolent influence of the Nephilim endures in the form of demons, disembodied spirits of the fallen giants. These malevolent entities seek to perpetuate the nefarious agenda that began with the Nephilim, tormenting and deceiving humanity throughout history.

Grey Aliens

Next is the Grey Aliens—enigmatic visitors from beyond. In contemporary narratives, the Grey Aliens emerge as enigmatic beings associated with extraterrestrial encounters. Accounts of alleged abductions and close encounters with these entities have fueled speculation and intrigue. Their motives and origins remain shrouded in mystery, adding to the allure of the unknown.

The Nordics—Mythical and Alluring Visitors

In the realm of extraterrestrial encounters, the Nordics are enigmatic beings described as tall, human-like entities with fair features. Tales of their interaction with humans evoke wonder and curiosity. Yet, their intentions and existence remain elusive, blending mythology with contemporary reports.

Conclusion

As we explore the world of bad seeds, encompassing the Nephilim, hybrid offspring, animal-human blending, demonic spirits of giants, Grey Aliens, and Nordics, we are confronted with a realm of mysteries and uncertainties. These tales of enigmatic beings and unholy creations caution us against straying from God's divine plan and the sanctity of life.

From ancient narratives to contemporary encounters, the presence of these entities challenges our understanding of reality and our place in the universe. As we navigate these enigmatic stories, may we remain steadfast in our faith and discernment, seeking to uphold righteousness and truth amidst the allure of the unknown.

While the mysteries of these entities persist, let us find solace in the unwavering light of God's truth and the divine order. As we confront the enigmatic allies and unsettling beings, may we be shielded from deception and malevolence, standing firm against all that defies the divine will. In this pursuit, may we find courage, wisdom, and discernment, relying on God's guidance and protection as we navigate the enigmatic world of the bad seeds.

So as we continue to investigate what has been happening since the beginning of time, may this bring us new revelations and understanding as we seek to uphold righteousness and live in alignment with God's divine order. As we face the giants and challenges in our own lives, may we draw strength from God's wisdom, recognizing that we are in a seed war that the enemy started and we must expose. Once the church understands this, we will not be deceived as God's people. Because the modern-day church has had such a limited view of the supernatural, it has kept many people from seeing the battle that has continued to rage right before our very eyes.

5

Seeds of Deception

UFO/UAP and Hidden Technologies
A Message of Hope

On July 26, 2023, history took a profound turn as the halls of Congress hosted a riveting hearing on Unidentified Aerial Phenomena (UAPs). The event brought to light astonishing revelations from three courageous Pentagon whistleblowers, David Grusch, Ryan Graves, and David Fravor, who stood before the nation to unveil a gripping truth: alien craft defying the laws of physics were among us, and the government held dark secrets.

This hearing is one of the most significant events in human history and marks a pivotal moment in the quest for UFO transparency. The House Oversight Committee became the epicenter of this momentous gathering. The trio of whistleblowers shared their harrowing accounts of government secrecy, revealing the suppression of vital information surrounding UFOs.

Under oath, David Grusch, a former U.S. intelligence officer and Air Force veteran, fearlessly disclosed that his life had been threatened and he was ordered to remain silent about a covert government-run crashed UFO retrieval program. He spoke of colleagues injured while attempting to reverse-engineer extraterrestrial technology concealed by shadowy figures within the government.

The three witnesses, Grusch, Graves, and Fravor, faced lawmakers' probing questions during the hearing. The hearing delved into decades of alleged government cover-ups concerning UFOs or UAPs, now referred to as Unidentified Anomalous Phenomena. As each witness testified, the world was left with a profound sense of urgency to confront the veil of secrecy.

Though constrained from divulging specifics in an open forum due to an ongoing whistleblower reprisal program case, Grusch asserted his readiness to share classified details with lawmakers.

Graves, a former F-18 pilot, provided firsthand accounts of close encounters with UAPs, describing their mind-bending abilities to accelerate, withstand hurricane-force winds, and outmaneuver U.S. fighter jets.

Fravor, a retired Navy pilot, recounted a chilling experience during a 2004 training mission, where he encountered the enigmatic "Tic Tac UFO," solidifying it as one of the most compelling pieces of evidence for UFO existence.

The whistleblowers' testimonies laid bare the unsettling reality of advanced UAPs that seemed to defy the laws of physics, exhibiting maneuvers beyond human comprehension, devoid of conventional propulsion systems and control surfaces. Their collective plea echoed loudly: end the government's stifling secrecy, unshackle the truth, and restore trust between the government and its citizens.

The hearing garnered bipartisan support, uniting political adversaries in the quest for UFO transparency. The Senate passed legislation to declassify and release UFO-related records, a pivotal step in bridging the gap between officialdom and the American people.

The nation was left grappling with the stark realization that UAPs posed not only a national security concern but also an aviation safety problem. Rep. Tim Burchett aptly remarked, "We can't trust a government that does not trust its people."

The fervor surrounding the UFO topic reached a boiling point, and it was David Grusch, a decorated Air Force veteran and intelligence officer, who catalyzed this momentous hearing. His brave decision to step into the spotlight became the catalyst that forced Congress to face the truth.

In the realm of UFO/UAP sightings and the pursuit of hidden technologies, we are confronted with mysteries and uncertainties that challenge our understanding of the world. As we explore concepts like Zero Point Energy, Electromagnetic Gravitics, and Consciousness-Assisted Technologies, we are met with questions about their potential to revolutionize our existence positively. However, there are powerful forces at play that wish to keep these advancements concealed.

Why is there such secrecy? The answer lies in the potential disruption these technologies could bring to established power structures and industries. Imagine a world where fossil fuels, pollution, and poverty are eradicated forever through the harnessing of advanced energy sources. Such a reality threatens the stronghold of global titans of industry and religious institutions, which may have hidden knowledge of ancient technologies, such as the building of the pyramids.

The true driving force behind the suppression of these technologies is not merely monetary gain but the control they provide over entire nations and their populations. The revelation of such advancements could lead to a shift in power dynamics, with centralized energy systems losing their grip on global governance. This potential loss of control fuels the efforts to keep these technologies hidden from the public eye.

In light of this secrecy, a great deception looms on the horizon, driven by media manipulation and fearmongering. The disclosure of UFO/UAP encounters, programmed life forms, abductions, hybrid breeding programs, as well as nuclear war, economic crashes, and food shortages may be used to instill fear and drive humanity toward a preconceived solution or savior. This eerily echoes themes found in Revelation and the prophesied return of giants.

Amidst these uncertainties and potential deceptions, Christians find hope in their faith and the promises of God. The foundation of Christianity lies in the belief in a loving and merciful God who has made promises of hope and redemption. Scriptures like Jeremiah 29:11 affirm God's plan for humanity's prosperity and well-being. This divine promise extends beyond individuals to encompass humanity as a whole.

The belief in the intrinsic value and dignity of every human being, as created in the image of God, inspires hope in our capacity for compassion and positive change. Throughout history, individuals and communities motivated by their Christian faith have demonstrated acts of love, selflessness, and courage, illuminating the potential for humanity to come together for the greater good.

Above all, Christians find solace in acknowledging God's sovereignty and ultimate victory over all creation. Trusting in God's plan, even amidst challenges, provides the confidence to face an uncertain future. Romans 8:28 assures believers that God works for the good of those who love Him, even in times of hardship.

As Christians navigate the complexities of hidden technologies, UFO/UAP encounters, and potential deceptions, they find hope in God's promises, the capacity for compassion within human hearts, and the assurance of God's sovereignty and final victory. Armed with this hope, Christians are empowered to face the future with confidence, actively seeking positive change and contributing to a better world for all. With God's spirit of power, love, and a sound mind within them, they overcome fear and embrace a future guided by hope and faith. As believers, they understand that "greater is He who is in you than he who is in the world" (John 4:4).

We believe this is one of the most historical moments in human history for the following reasons.

First, the shadows of secrecy and classified programs on this subject reveal an unsettling truth that the alien presence is not a mere conspiracy theory but a real and potentially significant national security threat. Testimonials from various sources reveal an intricate web of government entities, private companies, and military contractors engaged in covert activities involving alien craft and biological entities. We believe these are fallen angel technologies and demonic activities. As we peel back the layers of classified operations, communication with non-human entities, and the use of black budgets, we come face to face with a reality that challenges our understanding of the world and begins to reshape our understanding of the Hebrew Bible.

The Bible teaches us that there is nothing new under the sun. So let's take a look at some of the most recent disclosures in our current history.

Alien Craft and Biological Entities

For decades there have been whispers of secret projects involving alien technology and biological entities. These conversations have long circulated in the realm of so-called "conspiracy theories." However, testimonies from insiders and whistleblowers shed light on the actual existence of these covert operations. Elements of governments including military, private companies, and military contractors have reportedly obtained alien craft and biological entities, engaging in undisclosed activities to unravel the mysteries of their advanced technology. Behind closed doors, far from the public eye, scientists and engineers have been working to reverse engineer these extraterrestrial artifacts, potentially aiming to gain an edge in advanced aerospace capabilities.

Interactions with Non-Human Entities

Perhaps even more astonishing are claims of direct communication and collaboration with non-human entities. Testimonies suggest that contact with intelligent beings from beyond our planet has occurred, leading to exchanges of information and advanced technology that defy our understanding of the natural world. The nature of these interactions remains shrouded in mystery, raising profound questions about the existence of beings of extraterrestrial intelligence and their intentions toward humanity. We submit that these are fallen angels and their genetically created biologics.

Black Budgets and Unregulated Projects

The financial underpinning of these covert programs comes from black budgets—funds allocated for classified operations that evade public scrutiny and standard oversight. These unregulated projects operate in the shadows, without the checks and balances that typically govern government expenditures. The secrecy surrounding these financial allocations raises concerns about transparency and accountability, leaving the public largely unaware of the significant resources invested in these classified endeavors.

Threats and Intimidation

Maintaining secrecy about these classified operations is paramount to those involved, leading to reports of threats and intimidation directed at individuals who might divulge sensitive information. Witnesses who dare to share their experiences often face severe consequences, making it challenging for the truth to come to light. This culture of secrecy perpetuates a cycle of concealment, preventing public awareness and understanding of the potential national security implications of the alien presence.

The testimonies and examples presented here paint a sobering picture of the alien presence as a genuine national security concern. The involvement of elements within governments, private companies, and military contractors in the possession and reverse engineering of alien technology raises profound questions about the potential impact on global power dynamics and security interests.

The communication with non-human entities adds an enigmatic layer to the narrative, prompting us to explore the possibilities of extraterrestrial involvement and their intentions toward humanity. As we grapple with the implications of these encounters, the secrecy surrounding black budgets and unregulated projects compounds the challenge of understanding the full extent of these endeavors.

In the face of threats and intimidation, shedding light on these covert operations becomes an arduous task. Nevertheless, confronting the reality of the alien presence is crucial for national security and global interests. It calls for increased transparency, accountability, and ethical considerations in exploring and handling this delicate subject.

God's word clearly teaches us that His people perish for lack of knowledge. And in the last days there will be a great deception and falling away. We believe this is a continuation of the plan to defile the human condition and destroy the human family.

This is the seed wars!

6

The Digital Seeds

There is an undeniable reality that we are in the era of Genesis 6 all over again—the re-creation of hybrid humans. This raises profound questions about human identity, the boundaries of enhancement, societal impact, and the eternal consequences for the human soul. As a Christian and a scientist, we address the ethical, societal, and legal aspects of genetic engineering and modifying the human genome. This chapter explores the manufacture of artificial eggs and sperm cells, known as in vitro gametogenesis (IVG), which could potentially lead to the production of "designer babies."

While IVG offers hope for medically infertile individuals to have biologically related children, it also brings up concerns about other genetically modified biologics as well.

The aim is to ensure that the future of hybrid humans aligns with shared values and aspirations.

However, a counterargument emerges as this chapter takes a high-resolution look into the potential pitfalls and ethical dilemmas associated with using AI to create human hybrids. Here are five compelling arguments against pursuing such a path, supported by credible references:

1. Ethical Concerns

The creation of human hybrids through AI raises significant ethical questions about tampering with the fundamental aspects of human identity. According to the UNESCO Universal Declaration on Bioethics and Human Rights, "Practices which are contrary to human dignity, such as reproductive cloning of human beings, shall not be permitted."

2. Inequality and Discrimination

The introduction of AI-created human hybrids may exacerbate existing social inequalities. Access to advanced technologies may become limited to certain privileged groups, resulting in discrimination and a deeper divide between the wealthy and the less privileged. As highlighted in a report by the World Economic Forum, "Emerging technologies could exacerbate inequalities among individuals and communities if they are not governed with the public interest in mind."

3. Unpredictable Long-Term Consequences

The long-term effects of creating AI-driven human hybrids are uncertain and potentially irreversible. Genetic modifications could lead to unintended genetic mutations or unforeseen health implications for future generations. A study published in Nature Biotechnology warns about the potential for "off-target effects and unintended consequences" when using gene-editing technologies like CRISPR.

4. Loss of Human Authenticity and Diversity

AI-driven human hybrids may lead to a homogenized society, where individuality and diversity are compromised. The uniqueness of human experiences, emotions, and characteristics could be overshadowed by standardized genetic enhancements. The American Medical Association states that "Genetic enhancement that does not address any specific disease or disability raises the question of whether society is accepting, endorsing, and fostering the notion that the human species could and should be improved."

5. Spiritual and Moral Considerations

The creation of AI-driven human hybrids poses spiritual and moral dilemmas for various religious and philosophical beliefs. Many religions advocate for the sanctity of life and the belief that human beings are created in the image of a higher power. Theologians and ethicists have expressed concerns about "playing god" and the potential consequences on the human soul and moral fabric of society.

Conclusion

In conclusion, while AI and genetic engineering show promise for various aspects of human life, the creation of human hybrids through AI raises profound ethical, social, and moral questions. "The Digital Seeds" calls for thoughtful dialogue, consideration of credible research, and ethical guidelines to assess the potential long-term consequences before venturing into uncharted territories that may redefine what it means to be human.

But one thing is certain, the intrusion of artificial intelligence into our lives remains as subtle as a thief in the night. These "Digital Seeds" will continue weaving themselves seamlessly into the fabric of our daily existence, often leaving us oblivious to its agenda…the Nephilim agenda! In the profoundly insightful words of Joe Allen, an author and theologian, "Transhumanism marks the epochal fusion of humanity and Machine. A current epoch marked by billions wielding smartphones paves the way for an imminent era where our minds intertwine with artificial intelligence networks."

With uncanny parallels to the modern mythos, the world-renowned robot entity known as Sophia emerges as an embodiment of a burgeoning techno-religion. Her nomenclature draws from the deity—or Aeon—whose descent from grace is chronicled within the enigmatic Gnostic Gospels.

Possessing an erudite grounding in the realms of both science and theology, Allen grapples with the enigma encapsulated by what he dubs "upright souls birthing a digital monstrosity." Through the profound literary journey offered in his book Dark Aeon, Allen casts a spotlight on humanity's very essence. It is a symphony that resonates through the annals of history, delving into the inception of Scientism, traversing the expanse to our era of government-sanctioned mRNA vaccines, and even peering into the surreal aspirations of cybernetic tycoons like Elon Musk.

Across the vast landscapes of Silicon Valley to the distant corners of China, the aspirations of these global visionaries—laid bare and expounded upon in Dark Aeon—loom with an aura of impending doom and dread. Yet, Allen is unwavering in his assertion that the salvation of humanity rests within our grasp. And we assert that this is a continuation of the Genesis 6 seed wars in which the enemy is trying to defile the human genome. We must not only recognize this threat, but we must confront and not allow our humanity to be defiled and destroyed!

References:

- Allen, Joe. Dark Aeon: Navigating the Intersection of Humanity and Technology.

- Gnostic Gospels. Reference to Aeon and symbolism.

- Musk, Elon. The Visionary Quest: Technological Horizons.

- Scientism and Its Impact: Exploring the Dynamics of Modern Science.
- UNESCO. Universal Declaration on Bioethics and Human Rights. Retrieved from: https://unesdoc.unesco.org/ark:/48223/pf0000144556
- World Economic Forum. The Global Risks Report 2021. Retrieved from: https://www.weforum.org/reports/the-global-risks-report-2021
- Doudna, J. A., & Charpentier, E. (2014). Genome editing. The new frontier of genome engineering with CRISPR-Cas9. Science, 346(6213), 1258096. doi:10.1126/science.1258096
- American Medical Association. Genetic Enhancement. Retrieved from: https://www.ama-assn.org/delivering-care/ethics/genetic-enhancement
- Turner, R. (2015). Theological and Ethical Perspectives on Human Enhancement. In M. J. Cherry & M. J. Cherry (Ed.), Persons and their Bodies: Rights, Responsibilities, Relationships (pp. 161-176). Springer. doi:10.1007/978-94-017-9917-5_13

7
Giants of Yore

Throughout human history, stories of giant beings have persisted across cultures and continents. Written and oral accounts of giants, like the towering titans of antiquity, evoke a sense of awe and wonder. But one question must be asked.

Were the giants of Genesis 6 only on the earth in the days of antiquity?

Our answer is a resounding *NO!*

Though in the Western world, we are taught that these giants are myth and legend, evidence of these ancient giants is not confined solely to the realm of tall tales. Throughout the world, tantalizing traces of enormous skeletal remains have been discovered, raising questions about the possibility of their existence and the mysteries they hold.

The stories and testimonies span the globe. From the Nephilim of biblical accounts to the Greek Titans and Norse Jotnar, tales of giants populate every corner of the earth. These stories often depict giants as powerful, imposing figures that once dominated the earth.

Their extraordinary stature and strength captured the imagination of ancient civilizations. While interpretations of these Titans vary, the idea of divine beings intermingling with humans, giving rise to a race of giants, endures as a captivating narrative.

But what about the bones? Are giant skeletons fact or fiction?

The quest for evidence of giants has led to the discovery of enormous skeletal remains in various parts of the world. Often shrouded in controversy, these finds have ignited debates about their authenticity. In the 19th and early 20th centuries, reports emerged of giant bones unearthed during construction and excavation projects worldwide. Interestingly, when giant bones are unearthed, the government, Smithsonian, and even the Vatican always seem to confiscate them and discredit their authenticity very quickly.

Despite skepticism, several discoveries have sparked intrigue and warrant closer examination. In the mid-20th century, amateur archaeologist Jim Vieira began researching accounts of giant skeletons in North America. His investigations led to the documented discovery of oversized skeletal remains in mounds and burial sites across the continent.

Modern researchers in the fields of archaeology and cryptozoology have taken up the mantle of investigating giant-related claims as well. Archaeologists, equipped with advanced tools and methodologies, seek to separate fact from fiction. On the other hand, cryptozoologists delve into the possibility of undiscovered or extinct creatures that could explain giant legends.

In Ecuador, the "Los Tayos Caves" captured the world's attention in the 1970s when explorers claimed to have found a complex underground network containing chambers with oversized skeletal remains. While these claims faced criticism, they underscore the allure of the unknown and the quest to decipher humanity's past. Again, we submit to you that the history of our earth is very different from what we have been taught.

Advancements in science have allowed researchers to explore these claims with greater precision. Radiocarbon dating, isotopic analysis, and genetic studies have helped shed light on the authenticity of these giant remains. Despite the potential for manipulation and misidentification, some analyses have yielded intriguing results.

One such example is the discovery of elongated skulls in Peru. These skulls, elongated through cultural practices such as cranial head-boarding or genetic factors, have fueled speculation about ancient populations that might have given rise to giant legends. Genetic testing has offered insights into the origins of these skulls, but the true extent of their connection to giants is still under investigation.

The quest to unveil the truth behind giants and their colossal remains is one that continues to captivate the imagination. As technology advances, the lines between legend and reality blur, offering the potential to separate fact from fiction. While many discoveries have been debunked or remain unverified, the tantalizing possibility of uncovering evidence of a lost chapter of our past remains a driving force for both researchers and enthusiasts.

In this age of exploration and discovery, the giants of old remain enigmatic symbols of human curiosity and our unquenchable thirst for knowledge and truth. Whether destined to remain in the realm of myth or poised to emerge from the shadows of history, the giants of antiquity continue to leave an indelible mark on the tapestry of our understanding.

One thing is certain, we must all face the giants!

8
Clash of the Titans

In this chapter, we will take a 20,000-foot view into the captivating world of Greek mythology. We will focus on the Titans and their epic clash with the Olympian gods and draw parallels between Greek legends and the ancient Hebrew Bible narrative of fallen angels and Nephilim. We will look closer at the intriguing connections between these hybrids of antiquity and the mythological entities that have been passed down through written and oral traditions across cultures.

The historical landscape of ancient Greece is preserved with tales of powerful deities and their interactions with humanity. Among these figures, the Titans stand as primordial beings who once ruled over the cosmos. This chapter delves into their tumultuous relationship with the Olympian gods and examines how these narratives intertwine with the stories of fallen angels and their enigmatic offspring, the Nephilim.

In Greek mythology, the Titans were ancient and formidable beings, representing the fundamental forces of the universe. Their dominion was characterized by both order and chaos, as they struggled for supremacy against their own kin and, later, against the Olympian gods. Among the most notable Titans were Cronus, Rhea, Hyperion, and Atlas. Their collective power, along with their intricate family dynamics, shaped the mythological tapestry of ancient Greece. The most prominent Titans included:

Cronus: The leader of the Titans and the youngest son of Uranus and Gaia. He overthrew his father and ruled until he was eventually overthrown by his own son, Zeus.

Rhea: The sister and wife of Cronus. She was the mother of the Olympian gods Zeus, Hera, Poseidon, Hades, Demeter, and Hestia.

Oceanus: The Titan god of the ocean, often depicted as a river that encircled the world.

Hyperion: The Titan associated with light and the sun.

Prometheus: A Titan known for his intelligence and for giving fire to humanity, which led to his punishment by Zeus.

The rise of the Olympian gods marked a pivotal shift in the cosmic order. Led by Zeus, the king of the gods, the Olympians challenged the dominion of the Titans. The ensuing conflict, known as the Titanomachy, or "The Clash of the Titans" depicted a celestial struggle between old and new gods, embodying themes of rebellion, power dynamics, and cosmic upheaval. The Olympians' victory ushered in a new era, where the gods held dominion over the mortal realm. The major Olympian gods included:

Zeus: The king of the gods, ruler of the sky and thunder.

Hera: The queen of the gods and the goddess of marriage and family.

Poseidon: The god of the sea and earthquakes.

Hades: The god of the underworld and the ruler of the dead.

Demeter: The goddess of agriculture and fertility.

Hestia: The goddess of the hearth and home.

Aphrodite: The goddess of love and beauty.

Apollo: The god of music, poetry, prophecy, and healing.

Artemis: The goddess of the hunt, wilderness, and childbirth.

Ares: The god of war.

Athena: The goddess of wisdom, courage, and strategic warfare.

Hermes: The messenger of the gods and the god of commerce, travel, and thieves.

These are just a few examples of the Titans and Olympians in Greek mythology. The pantheon was rich with various gods, goddesses, and mythological beings, each with their own unique roles and stories.

Now this is where we bring biblical history and ancient history together. Drawing parallels between the Titans and fallen angels reveals a profound connection. A very interesting infusion emerges in their shared defiance against established divine orders. Just as the Titans rebelled against the cosmic order set by the Titans, fallen angels defied the authority of the divine creator of the Hebrew Bible. The Titans' fall from grace and the angels' expulsion from heaven mirror themes of consequences for disobedience and the perilous pursuit of autonomy. These parallel narratives reflect humanity's age-old fascination with the consequences of challenging divine authority.

As we have detailed in the previous chapters regarding the Nephilim—the offspring of fallen angels and mortal women—the Titans bore children who bridged the gap between divine and mortal realms. The Nephilim, often interpreted as giants or beings of immense power, evoke curiosity about the interactions between different planes of existence. This parallel underscores the hybrid nature of the

Titans' progeny and their significant roles in shaping mythological narratives and oral traditions. The presence of such hybrid beings challenges conventional boundaries and invites contemplation of the complex relationships between gods and humans.

The "Clash of the Titans" and the fall of the Titans signify transitions in cosmic order, akin to the biblical narrative of the fallen angels. These historical events raise questions about the nature of power, rebellion, and divine intervention. Exploring these themes enriches our understanding of human perception of the divine and the consequences of crossing boundaries. It prompts consideration of the delicate balance between cosmic forces and the repercussions of disrupting that balance and disobeying the Most High!

Renowned scholars such as Mircea Eliade and Joseph Campbell have highlighted the universal appeal of such narratives. They emphasize how these stories reflect human aspirations, struggles, and relationships with the divine. By examining these possibilities across cultures, we gain insight into the shared human need to understand our place and purpose in this world. These universal motifs serve as bridges between diverse belief systems, transcending cultural barriers.

The interplay between Greek mythology and the biblical narratives underscores the versatility of stories as a means of expressing complex ideas. These narratives, while rooted in different cultures, share common threads that resonate with fundamental human experiences, encouraging contemplation of our history, our existence and the divine. The fusion of myth and truth enables individuals to grapple with profound existential questions through storytelling.

The clash of the Titans, as well as the fallen angels' rebellion, continues to inspire literature, art, and cultural conversations.

Modern interpretations of these narratives often highlight the enduring relevance of themes such as power dynamics, the consequences of hybrid experiments, artificial intelligence and the ever-present interplay between the divine and the mortal. These age-old narratives find new life in contemporary discussions about morality, power, and the human condition.

Expanding the scope of these parallels, many Native American tribes from the Northeast and Southwest still relate the legends of the red-haired giants and how their ancestors fought terrible, protracted wars against the giants when they first encountered them in North America. Others, like the Aztecs and Mayans, recorded their encounters with a race of giants to the north when they ventured out on exploratory expeditions. These accounts add another layer of interconnectedness between diverse mythologies.

We have delved into the enthralling saga of the Titans, their conflict with the Olympian gods, and the intriguing parallels drawn between Greek mythology and Judeo-Christian narratives found throughout the Hebrew Bible as well as other historical texts like the Book of Enoch. As these mythological entities resonate across cultures and time periods, they remind us of the universal human fascination with the divine, rebellion, and the intricate tapestry of existence.

9

The Mixing of Seeds

In Daniel 2, we encounter the famous dream of Nebuchadnezzar, a vision that some believe holds the key to understanding Gentile history and, ultimately, divine intervention. The dream's imagery—the comprising of various metals—has long been a subject of fascination and biblical prophecy. Even our everyday expression, "the idol has feet of clay," finds its roots in this classic passage.

But let's look deeper into the symbolism. What, exactly, does the "miry clay" in this vision represent? It appears to be an enigmatic mixture, somewhat intermingled with the iron. The term "miry clay" points to clay made from dust, a biblical idiom often associated with death. When Daniel interprets this element for us, he drops a cryptic statement in verse 43:

> And whereas thou sawest iron mixed with miry clay, they shall mingle themselves with the seed of men: but they shall not cleave one to another, even as iron is not mixed with clay.
>
> Daniel 2:43 (KJV)

Notice the shift to a personal pronoun, "they shall mingle themselves with the seed of men..." This choice of words raises intriguing questions, particularly when we consider the warning of Jesus in Luke 17:26, which inevitably brings us back to Genesis 6.

> And just as it happened in the days of Noah, so will it also be in the days of the Son of Man:

What, or who, could be mingling with the seed of men? It would seem to suggest beings who are distinct from the seed of men. Could this allude to a resurgence of the hybrid breeding program that Genesis 6 hints at? The implications are profound, especially when viewed in the context of future global governance and the agenda to defile the human genome. Could these enigmatic "aliens" form a significant political constituency?

Might we witness UFO incidents as part of a meticulously orchestrated agenda to lead us toward a specific political goal? Or could this already be unfolding before our eyes? Are the public disclosures, sightings of UFOs and the increasingly prevalent reports of abductions part of the groundwork for a broader narrative?

A growing concern within the psychiatric community revolves around the bizarre and alarmingly frequent reports of individuals claiming to have been "abducted" by occupants of UFOs. These accounts are too outlandish to readily accept, and yet they are too widespread and consistent to dismiss entirely. What is particularly unsettling is that national polls estimate that up to 3% of the population may be involved in such experiences.

Dr. John E. Mack, a prominent figure in this field and a professor of psychiatry at The Cambridge Hospital, Harvard Medical School, has garnered attention for his work. With over 150 articles in professional, peer-reviewed journals and a Pulitzer Prize, he possesses impressive credentials. Dr. Mack has personally investigated nearly a hundred abduction cases and has raised eyebrows in his profession by suggesting that these beings may indeed be real and that they may have an agenda centered around the development of a hybrid race. At a professional conference on abductions held at M.I.T., Dr. Mack posed a thought-provoking question: "If what these abductees are saying is happening to them isn't happening, then what is?" Could all of this be a revival of the peculiar events reminiscent of "the Days of Noah"?

As we venture into the intricate world of biblical prophecy, symbolism, and the perplexing realm of UFO phenomena, we find ourselves at the crossroads of ancient wisdom and modern mystery, contemplating the profound possibilities of our existence. The journey ahead is one of both revelation and inquiry, and it beckons us to explore the unknown with open minds and discerning hearts.

And always remember the most important thing is not to fear the seed of the enemy but to keep your gaze on the greatest seed of all, Jesus Christ, for He is the Final Seed!

10

The Final Seed

In the hallowed echoes of Genesis, an age-old prophecy unfolds, revealing a world poised on the precipice of an epic battle, a clash destined to resound through the annals of history, a battle between the eternal forces of good and evil. Just as the sacred text foretold the birth of the Messiah, the seed of hope, it also warned of the rise of a spirit of antichrist, the seed of Satan.

This cataclysmic confrontation transcends the mere realm of earthly conflicts, for the antichrist spirit is no ordinary adversary. It is a fallen angelic-human hybrid, empowered by the sinister forces of darkness, and wielding occult knowledge that would ensnare hearts and minds, deceiving and defiling many.

The world watches, transfixed by a mixture of fascination and dread, as the antichrist spirit's influence spreads like a virulent contagion. Its promises of dominion, wealth, and a new world order captivate the masses, obscuring the true nature of its intentions—the annihilation of God's beings created in His own image. Its deception is masterful, ensnaring even the most discerning minds.

Yet amid the encroaching darkness, we, the Ekklesia, the believers in Christ, hold the ultimate hope. Ancient prophecies whisper in the hearts of those who refuse the antichrist spirit's allure. A new assembly of believers emerges, armed not with conventional weapons but with unwavering faith and an unyielding resolve to stand for the one true God.

We must recognize that our battle transcends the physical realm, delving into the unseen, demanding spiritual weaponry and divine intervention. Armed with prayer, scripture, and an unbreakable connection to our Creator, we embark on a mission to unveil the antichrist spirit's true nature and awaken the world to the impending great deception.

This deception is the reign of the Final Nephilim, who is tightening its grip on the world's institutions, economies, and ideologies. Yet, believers' faith remains unshaken, grounded in the age-old truth that the Light of the World can never be overcome by darkness.

In a moment that reverberates throughout the cosmos, the heavens part, and an overwhelming radiance pierces through the shadows. Celestial beings descend, heralded by the blare of trumpets and the earth's tremor beneath their weight.

> For the Lord Himself will descend from heaven with a shout, with the voice of the archangel and with the trumpet of God, and the dead in Christ will rise first. Then we who are alive, who remain, will be caught up together with them in the clouds to meet the Lord in the air, and so we will always be with the Lord.
>
> 1 Thessalonians 4:16–17

Now at that time Michael, the great prince who stands guard over the sons of your people, will arise. And there will be a time of distress such as never occurred since there was a nation until that time; and at that time your people, everyone who is found written in the book, will be rescued. And many of those who sleep in the dust of the ground will awake, these to everlasting life, but the others to disgrace and everlasting contempt.

Daniel 12:1–2

And then the sign of the Son of Man will appear in the sky, and then all the tribes of the earth will mourn, and they will see the Son of Man coming on the clouds of the sky with power and great glory. And He will send forth His angels with a great trumpet blast, and they will gather together His elect from the four winds, from one end of the sky to the other.

Matthew 24:30–31

Behold, I am telling you a mystery; we will not all sleep, but we will all be changed, in a moment, in the twinkling of an eye, at the last trumpet; for the trumpet will sound, and the dead will be raised imperishable, and we will be changed. For this perishable must put on the imperishable, and this mortal must put on immortality.

1 Corinthians 15:51–53

Jesus Christ returns, and His presence ignites a love and authority that shatters the illusions of the deceit of the antichrist spirit.

The final showdown unfolds on a grand cosmic stage, where the forces of darkness clash head-on with the brilliance of the ultimate Truth embodied by Christ. The antichrist spirit's dark incantations and deceptive schemes crumble before the radiance of this Truth. With a triumphant cry, the voices of believers join in chorus with His, and the reign of the Final Nephilim comes to a crushing end!

The world, bruised and broken, awakens from the shackles of deception, finally comprehending the truth of a conflict prophesied since the dawn of time—a conflict not waged with conventional arms but with the boundless power of faith, love, and the return of the one true Messiah. The Final Seed, sown in the soil of human existence, has risen to bring forth the harvest of salvation.

As we navigate the ever-darkening labyrinth of the Final Seed's reign:

➢ *Remember* the words of Genesis 3:15.

> And I will make enemies
> Of you and the woman,
> And of your offspring and her Descendant;
> He shall bruise you on the head,
> And you shall bruise Him on the heel.

➢ *Cling to* the promise of 1 John 2:18.

> Children, it is the last hour; and just as you heard that antichrist is coming, even now many antichrists have appeared; from this we know that it is the last hour.

➢ *Heed* the warning of Matthew 24:24.

> For false christs and false prophets will arise and will provide great signs and wonders, so as to mislead, if possible, even the elect.

➢ *Embrace* the spiritual battle described in Ephesians 6:12.

> For our struggle is not against flesh and blood, but against the rulers, against the powers, against the world forces of this darkness, against the spiritual forces of wickedness in the heavenly places.

➢ *Hold fast* to the triumphant return depicted in Revelation 19:11–16.

> And I saw heaven opened, and behold, a white horse, and He who sat on it is called Faithful and True, and in righteousness He judges and wages war. His eyes are a

flame of fire, and on His head are many crowns; and He has a name written on Him which no one knows except Himself. He is clothed with a robe dipped in blood, and His name is called The Word of God. And the armies which are in heaven, clothed in fine linen, white and clean, were following Him on white horses. From His mouth comes a sharp sword, so that with it He may strike down the nations, and He will rule them with a rod of iron; and He treads the wine press of the fierce wrath of God, the Almighty. And on His robe and on His thigh He has a name written: "KING OF KINGS, AND LORD OF LORDS."

In these truths, we find our strength, our purpose, and our unwavering hope, for as John 1:5 proclaims,

> The Light shines in the darkness
> and the darkness did not grasp it.

Part II
Further Evidence

11

Where Have All the Bones Gone?

> That which has been is that which will be, And that which has been done is that which will be done. So there is nothing new under the sun. Is there anything of which one might say, "See this, it is new?" Already it has existed for ages which were before us. There is no remembrance of earlier things; and also of the later things which will occur, there will be for them no remembrance among those who will come later still.
>
> Ecclesiastes 1:9–11

Over the centuries, enormous bones have been discovered on Earth, sparking excitement and speculation worldwide. These findings were widely publicized in newspapers. However, by the 1930s, they began to fade from public view due to a secretive censorship campaign. Since then, almost every unearthed skeleton has vanished under mysterious circumstances. Whenever gigantic bones are found, authorities such as the government, the Smithsonian, and even the Vatican swiftly remove them from public display and erase them from public knowledge. Their goal is to promote a worldview that is more mythical than fundamental to the public.

The quest for evidence of giant beings has long been a source of fascination and controversy. Reports of massive skeletons have surfaced throughout history, only to be removed from official records or dismissed as myths. This chapter explores the mysterious history of giant bones, the theories about their disappearance, and what these stories reveal about our understanding of biblical history, mythology, and a potential cover-up involving giants.

The allure of giant bones dates back to ancient civilizations. Greek and Roman scholars like Herodotus and Pliny the Elder documented these gigantic skeletons unearthed by natural forces or hidden in caves. Herodotus recounted the discovery of a giant's remains in what is now Turkey. At the same time, Pliny mentioned immense bones found in India, attributing them to the legendary Titans. These accounts often lacked detailed documentation and verifiable evidence despite their fascinating nature. *Or did they?*

> It is the glory of God to conceal a matter, and the glory of kings to investigate a matter.
>
> Proverbs 25:2 (ISV)

The 19th century brought renewed interest in giant bones with the rise of paleontology and archaeology. Large bones and skeletal remains claimed to belong to giants captivated the public and the scientific community. In 1838, a large femur was reported near Vicksburg, Mississippi, supposedly belonging to a nearly twelve-foot-tall human. Similarly, in 1868, the New York Times covered the discovery of giant skeletons in an Ohio mound, allegedly over ten feet tall. Despite the initial excitement, these findings were seldom subjected to rigorous scientific examination and soon disappeared from public view. This thought pattern would become the pattern even to the modern day.

Where Have All the Bones Gone?

One of the most infamous cases is the Cardiff Giant, discovered in 1869 in Cardiff, New York. Initially claimed to be a petrified prehistoric man, the giant's remains were later exposed as a carved gypsum block. This scandal cast a long shadow over other credible giant bone discoveries, leading to heightened skepticism and scrutiny of ensuing finds.

However, biblical scholars and the public did not dismiss all reports of giant bones quickly. In the early 20th century, the "Giant of Castelnau" emerged in France. Large human-like bones were discovered in a gravel pit near Castelnau. Renowned scientists of the time, including the French anthropologist Édouard Lartet, reportedly examined these bones and concluded they belonged to a race of giants. Yet, the bones eventually disappeared, leaving only scant records and speculative accounts. This disappearance has fueled speculation about whether the bones were actually removed, lost, or deliberately hidden.

Several theories attempted to explain why so many giant bones have vanished. One theory posits that the bones were lost or destroyed due to inadequate preservation techniques. In the 19th and early 20th centuries, excavation methods were often rudimentary, and scientific standards for documentation were less rigorous than today. Valuable specimens might have been discarded or misplaced during hurried or poorly managed excavations. Early scientists, lacking modern preservation tools, may have unintentionally allowed significant finds to deteriorate or be lost.

Another theory suggests deliberate suppression. Groundbreaking discoveries often need more support from established scientific platforms. The existence of giants, however, challenges conventional understandings of human evolution and prehistoric life. Some argue that evidence of giants might have been dubious to preserve the dominance of prevailing scientific theories. Reluctance to embrace controversial ideas can lead to the suppression of evidence that does not align with established paradigms, including religious establishments.

Folklore and mythology also play a role in shaping perceptions of giant bones. Many cultures have oral traditions and stories about giants, from the Nephilim in the Bible to the Jotnar in the Norse. Discoveries of unusually large bones may have been interpreted through these cultural lenses, leading to exaggerated claims and misunderstandings. Myths and legends could have influenced how these reported discoveries were perceived, blending elements of fact with fiction. But let us allow ourselves to recount the biblical stories of giants and their impact on the human race.

Modern archaeology and paleontology now offer new tools and methods that could potentially unravel some of these mysteries. Advances in DNA analysis, radiocarbon dating, and three-dimensional imaging provide opportunities to reexamine historical claims more precisely. Yet, historical records are often incomplete, and physical evidence is frequently missing, degraded or worse, hidden! The challenge lies in reconstructing the past from fragments and filling in the gaps left by lost or destroyed specimens.

The persistence of giant bone claims intersects with contemporary alternative theories and pseudoscience. The idea of ancient giants is a recurring theme throughout the ancient world, which proposes advanced prehistoric civilizations or extraterrestrial influences. These theories often use historical claims of giant bones as evidence, but where are the bones? The endurance of such ideas reflects a deep human fascination with the extraordinary, the unknown, and, most importantly, the unseen realm.

In conclusion, the quest to understand the giant bones of history reveals a complex interplay of discovery, myth, scientific inquiry and a biblical understanding of the Genesis 6 narrative. While some claims may stem from hoaxes or misidentifications, others remain shrouded in mystery due to lost, hidden and even destroyed evidence. The challenge is in uncovering the truth behind these bones and understanding how biblical understanding, human imagination, historical records, and scientific progress intersect. As technology advances and discoveries emerge, the hope remains that the enigma of the giants might one day be resolved, offering new insights into our distant past and the biblical narrative that has shaped the understanding of those who are open to seeing the truth.

12

The Giants of North America

As we delve into the topic of the giants of North America, we are not referring to the New York Giants football team, led by Eli Manning to two Superbowl victories, or to the San Francisco Giants baseball team, which has hosted great record-breaking players like Willie Mays, Barry Bonds, Will Clark, and George Burns (not the cigar-smoking comedian; he was really funny). Instead, we are focusing on ancient giants of much larger physical stature, who were likely much meaner and uglier (though we have our doubts about Lawrence Taylor).

There is much heated debate among independent researchers, academics, and skeptics about the origins of the North American giants. However, recent improvements in data collection and analysis advancements have laid the groundwork for more thorough research into this mesmerizing topic. Additionally, there is convincing evidence to indicate that the giants may have had their roots within the Americas.

Many Native American creation myths and oral histories mention giants from ancient times. One such example can be found in the book *Six Nations* (1825) by Tuscarora Indian

David Cusick. He writes that when the Great Spirit created the people, some of them turned into giants.

However, most people don't believe in giants and instead dismiss the idea as folklore sensationalized by newspaper journalists. We disagree. There is evidence in Native American mythology, genetic data, ethnological studies, scientific reports, early excavation records, first-hand accounts, and discoveries featured in newspapers and town history books to suggest otherwise. Now is the time for academia to examine this data and investigate what really happened at the Smithsonian, as an essential chapter in human history is at risk of being lost forever.

The oral traditions of various Native American tribes, including the Iroquois, Osage, Tuscaroras, Hurons, and Omahas, all contain accounts of enormous individuals who purportedly inhabited their ancestral lands. Across the contemporary United States, these stories persist as evidence of the existence of these ancient giants.

Records from various sources such as newspaper accounts, town and county histories, letters, scientific journals, diaries, photos, and Smithsonian ethnology reports have meticulously documented the unearthing of over 1,000 seven-foot and taller skeletons from ancient burial sites in North America over 200 years. These remarkable discoveries span coast to coast and reveal intriguing anatomical anomalies, including double rows of teeth, exceptionally large jawbones, and elongated skulls. These findings have been extensively recorded in nearly every state, sparking curiosity and further investigation into the origins and significance of these strange remains.

The Giants of North America

In the annual reports of the Smithsonian, scientists have meticulously identified at least 17 skeletons that were found to be over seven feet in height. Among these specimens, one astonishing example measured an impressive 8 feet tall. Additionally, the reports documented the discovery of a skull with a remarkable 36-inch circumference in Anna, Illinois, as recorded in the Smithsonian Annual Report of 1873. This is particularly noteworthy as the average human skull typically has a circumference of about 20 inches. Furthermore, historical records demonstrate that the Smithsonian Institution is cited multiple times as the recipient of gigantic skeletons unearthed from various locations across the United States. The skeletons mentioned no longer seem to exist, regardless of their actual size, and the remaining ones that were on display were removed and repatriated by NAGPRA (Native American Graves Protection and Repatriation Act).

Arkansas, USA

This account from an Ozark cave in Arkansas is found in The New Age Magazine (Volume 18, 1913), given by the highly regarded reporter Victor Schoffelmeyer.

In *Search for the Lost Giants*, a team of investigators explored the site of a cave that had been submerged due to the construction of Beaver Lake between 1960 and 1966. Bill Vieira and professional scuba diver Mike Young bravely dived into the waters of the lake, where they made an incredible discovery. They found a massive shelter cave that was believed to be the very place where the skeletal remains had been found. Upon further exploration, they came across a remarkable 70-foot stone wall at the cave entrance, indicating potential human habitation in the past. Although this was a significant finding, unfortunately, no additional clues or evidence emerged during their investigation. Below is an excerpt from the original article, which reads as follows:

> "While the historical features of the Ozarks held our attention, by far the most fascinating discovery was one made by an aged recluse and naturalist who for ten years had lived in a shelter cave near where we camped. "Dad" Riggins spent much of his time digging in the ashes which form the floor of many of these caves. At a depth of more than three feet he found the remains of several giant human skeletons, including an almost perfect skull which differed in many particulars from a modern specimen. When partly joined, the largest skeleton was almost ten feet tall. Dad Riggins showed us hieroglyphics covering the Palisades thought to be thousands of years old."

California, USA

> "In 1819, an old lady saw a gigantic skeleton dug up by soldiers at Purisima on the Lompock Rancho. The natives deemed it a god, and it was reburied by direction of the padre."

In 1833, a report emerged with more detailed information about an intriguing discovery. According to the story, soldiers were digging a pit for a powder magazine at Lompock Rancho, California, when they came across a layer of cemented gravel. They uncovered a 12-foot stone coffin containing the skeleton of a giant man, about twelve feet tall. The grave was surrounded by carved shells, enormous stone axes, two spears, and thin sheets of porphyry, a purple mineral with quartz, covering the skeleton. These artifacts were covered with unintelligible symbols. The giant man had a double row of teeth, both upper and lower. Upon consulting with a local tribe of Indians, who went into a trance, it was exclaimed that they were geographically displaced Allegewi Indians from the Ohio Valley area. When the natives began to attach religious significance to the discovery, a padre called for the skeleton and all the artifacts to be reburied.

Catalina Island, off the coast of California, has been the site of numerous discoveries of oversized skeletons. The story is intriguing and controversial, involving amateur archaeologist Ralph Glidden and his unusual museum. However, before Glidden's involvement, a German naturalist named Dr. A. W. Furstenan sparked the story in 1913 when he reported uncovering an 8-foot-tall skeleton on Catalina. The skeleton was found with artifacts such as mortar, pestles, and arrowheads. Dr. Furstenan had been told a legend while in Mexico about a giant and noble race that had lived on the island long before the arrival of the white man and had subsequently disappeared.

Amateur archaeologist Ralph Glidden contributed significantly to the story by unearthing and collecting a total of 3,781 skeletons on the Channel Islands between 1919 and 1930. While working for the Heye Foundation of New York, he unearthed a 9-foot-2-inch skeleton and several others measuring over 7 feet.

In 1895, there was a fascinating report on a giant mummy that was found in San Diego, California. It is currently believed to be a hoax. However, let's take a closer look, as this famous story has some intrigue and inconsistency. The initial report, which surfaced in 1895, featured sub-headings such as "Nine Feet High and Probably a California Indian" and "Measurement Well Authenticated. Other Big Men and Women of Fact and Fable Who Are Famous Types Of

Gigantism." After precise measurements were taken, the stature of the giant was found to be 8 feet 4 inches. These measurements were carefully inspected and verified by Prof. Thomas Wilson, who served as the Curator of the Department of Prehistoric Anthropology at the Smithsonian Institution, along with other scientists.

Thirteen years after its initial examination in 1908, the mummy was put on display at the Smithsonian. Following this, the Smithsonian conducted tests and promptly dismissed it as a hoax, claiming it was made of "gelatin." The significant time lapse, the $500 spent to acquire it, and the earlier "careful inspection" by experts suggest that there might be more to this story than initially assumed.

It's worth citing that a gentleman named Ales Hrdlicka joined the Smithsonian in 1903, right between the discovery and the eventual debunking of the giants. Mr. Hrdlicka wasn't interested in the giants and actively tried to remove them from the historical record. Additionally, Mr. Thomas Wilson, the Director of Prehistoric Anthropology, and Mr. W. J. McGee, the ethnologist in charge, were both involved in this story and were determined to bring the giants back to the Smithsonian headquarters, despite the hefty cost ($500 in 1895 is equivalent to $15,000 today). But why would they go to such lengths if it was just a hoax?

Iowa, USA

The following account is from The Worthington Advance (November 18, 1897). It describes the ethnological work of the Smithsonian Institution's Division of Eastern Mounds. The report quotes the Director of the Bureau of Ethnology at the time, John Wesley Powell. An image was also included with the news report.

> "It is a matter of official record that in digging through a mound in Iowa the scientists found the skeleton of a giant, who, judging from actual measurement, must have stood seven feet six inches tall when alive. The bones crumbled to dust when exposed to the air."
>
> The Worthington Advance
> (November 18, 1897)

Missouri, USA

As part of the Search for the Lost Giants show, Jim and fellow researcher James Clary investigated the following account that had this heading:

> "An Ancient Ozark Giant Dug Up Near Steelville: Strange discovery made by a boy looking for arrowheads, gives this Missouri Town an absorbing mystery to ponder.
>
> "…he turned up the complete skeleton of an 8 foot giant. The grisly find was brought to Dr. R. C. Parker here and stretched out to its enormous length in a hallway of his office where it has since remained the most startling exhibit Steelville has ever had on public view."
>
> From The Steelville Ledger
> June 11, 1933

Dr. R. C. Parker notes,

> "As I delved into the archives on microfilm at the Steelville library, I stumbled upon three detailed reports documenting an intriguing discovery."

The reports were accompanied by a captivating photograph capturing the moment when Les Eaton, a towering 6-foot figure, was sprawled next to an amazing 8-foot skeleton in Dr. Parker's office. According to the Steelville Ledger, the enigmatic skeleton was meticulously packed and shipped to the renowned Smithsonian Institution, vanishing into obscurity thereafter.

Ohio, USA

The Great Serpent Mound, a prehistoric model mound situated near Peebles, Ohio, extends to a length of 1,370 feet. It has been thoroughly examined by researcher Ross Hamilton, who has extensively covered its secrets and discovered giants in the region. According to a recent radiocarbon study, the mound dates back to around 321 BC, aligning with the period of the Adena civilization, which is believed to have been active in the area at that time.

In the 1890s, Professor Frederic Ward Putnam conducted excavations near the Serpent Mound, unearthing the skeletal remains of individuals measuring 6 feet in height. However, researcher Jeffrey Wilson recently unearthed a postcard featuring a 7-foot-tall skeleton. This postcard may depict one of the skeletons excavated by Putnam, as he was the sole individual to have undertaken archaeological digs at the site.

In his book, *A Tradition of Giants*, Ross initially presented this information, clearly stating that it was from Serpent Mound on the postcard. However, there still needs to be more debate surrounding the location where the photo of a 7 foot skeleton was taken. The legs are cut off at the knees, so the 7 foot measurement might be an estimation. The skeleton could have been closer to 8 feet tall if the lower legs and feet were attached.

The Miamisburg Mound, an ancient earthwork structure located in Miamisburg, Ohio, is believed to have been constructed by the Adena culture, a pre-Columbian Native American civilization, during the period of 1,000 to 200 BC. This conical burial mound is of great historical and archaeological significance, standing as the largest in Ohio. At its peak, the mound reached a towering height of almost 70 feet, which is equivalent to the height of a seven-story building and had a circumference of 877 feet.

An investigation was conducted at this historic site in September 2012. Researchers engaged with local researchers at the historical society and unearthed additional information indicating the presence of other skeletal remains in the surrounding area. This discovery further underscores the importance of the Miamisburg Mound as a site of interest for archaeological study and historical exploration.

Numerous skeletal remains, which included a giant jawbone and "bones of unusual size," were unearthed from the mound. However, the discovery was made half a mile away and captured national attention. The report, featured in The Middletown Signal on January 17, 1899, contains the following:

BONES OF PREHISTORIC GIANT FOUND NEAR MIAMISBURG

"The skeleton of a giant found near Miamisburg is the cause of much discussion not only among the curious and illiterate but among the learned scientists of the world. The body of a man more gigantic than any ever recorded in human history, has been found in the Miami Valley, in Ohio. The skeleton it is calculated must have belonged to a man 8 feet 1.5 inches in height."

From The Middletown Signal
January 17, 1899

Professor Thomas Wilson, a distinguished curator of prehistoric anthropology at the prestigious Smithsonian Institution, unequivocally affirmed the skull's unquestionable authenticity. He expounded on its significant antiquity, citing numerous similar crania unearthed in the Hopewell group of mounds in Ohio. Notably, he observed the jaws' prognathic nature and highlighted the specimen's remarkably low facial index.

Pennsylvania, USA

In 1870, in West Hickory, Pennsylvania, there was a report of an 18-foot skeleton that was said to have outdone the famous Cardiff Giant. This news was initially published in the Oil City Times. The report described some unusual anatomical components underneath the giant armor. It claimed that the skeleton was of staggering height, one of the tallest examples ever encountered.

> "They exhumed an enormous helmet of iron, which was corroded with rust. Further digging brought to light a sword which measured nine feet in length."

The article continued that they had discovered:

> "...a well-preserved skeleton of an enormous giant belonging to a species of the human family which probably inhabited this and other parts of the world at that time of which the Bible speaks...The bones of the skeleton are remarkably white. The teeth are all in their places, and all of them are double, and of extraordinary size."

The skeletal remains were said to stand at a towering 18 feet in height, sparking fascination and intrigue. However, skepticism arises regarding this accounting, as such a colossal size is unprecedented in historical records. The bones were in the process of being prepared for transport to New York. The discovery was reportedly made 12 feet underground within a mound, indicating a potentially ancient origin regardless of the actual height of the skeletal remains.

Tennessee

In 1845 and 1846, giant human bones were discovered in our home State of Tennessee. We have three accounts of this discovery for you to consider. The first two are newspaper articles from 1845 that report the findings of what were thought to be giant human remains. The third account, published in the American Journal of Science in 1846, provides a professional assessment of one set of these remains based on firsthand observation. The remains of "giant" creatures in this large category are not new or especially contentious.

Here is the first article from the Cleveland Herald on 10 September 1845.

A GIANT EXHUMED

"We are informed on the most reliable authority that a person in Franklin County, Tennessee, while digging a well, a few weeks since, found a human skeleton, at the depth of fifty feet, which measures eighteen feet in length. The immense frame was entire with an unimportant exception in one of the extremities. It has been visited by several of the principal members of the medical faculty in Nashville, and pronounced unequivocally, by all, the skeleton of a huge man. The bone of the thigh measured five feet; and it was computed that the height of the living man, making the proper allowance for muscles, must have been at least twenty feet. The finder had been offered eight thousand dollars for it, but had determined not to sell it any price until first exhibiting it for twelve months. He is now having the different parts wired together for this purpose. These unwritten records of the men and animals of other ages, that are from time to time dug out of the bowels of the earth, put conjecture to confusion, and almost surpass imagination itself."

Madison Banner.

The second account is from the New York Herald, the twelfth of December 1845.

THE GIANT SKELETON

"The skeleton discovered in Williamson county in this State, and supposed to be that of a human being, has frequently been referred to, within a few days past, in the House of Representatives. Notwithstanding the description given of it, as Wouter Van Twiller would say, "we have our doubts about the matter." This skeleton was found about sixty feet beneath the surface of the earth, embedded in a stratum of the hardest kind of clay. The bones are said to be in a perfect state of preservation, and weigh in the aggregate fifteen hundred pounds. All the large and characteristic bones are entire, and the skull, arms, and thigh bones, knee pans, shoulder sockets and collar bones remove all doubts, and the animal to whom they belonged has been decided "to belong to the genus homo." This gentleman, when he walked the earth, was about eighteen feet high, and when clothed in flesh must have weighed not less than 3000 pounds. "The bones of the thigh and leg measure six feet six inches; his skull is said to be about two-thirds the size of a flour barrel, and capable of holding in its cavities near two bushels. (He must have had a goodly quantity of brains, and if intellect be in proportion to the size of the brain, he must have possessed extraordinary intellectual powers). The description further states, that "a coffee cup of good size could be put in the eye-sockets." The jaw teeth weigh from 8 ½ to 6 pounds. It is stated that an eminent physician and anatomist is engaged in putting the skeleton together, and that it will shortly be ready for public exhibition."

Nashville Orthopolitan

In 1845, two separate accounts described similar discoveries of remains in different counties of Tennessee. Although the measurements of the femur differ, the estimated height of eighteen feet is the same in both accounts. The first account applies a "rule of thumb" that states the relationship between femur length and height, with height being four times the femur length, similar to the approach used for the Ellensburg skeleton.

The next quote is sourced from a paper authored by William M. Carpenter, which was published in the March 1846 issue (Volume 1, page 244) of the American Journal of Science.

> ART. XII.—Remarks on some Fossil Bones recently brought to New Orleans from Tennessee and from Texas; by William M. Carpenter, M.D., Prof. in the Med. Coll. of Louisiana.
>
> I. Fossils from Tennessee—the "gigantic Fossil Man," (being the skeleton of a young mastodon.) Much interest has been recently excited by the announcement of the discovery in Tennessee of the remains of a man eighteen feet high. The papers teemed with accounts of the prodigy, and public confidence was secured by the assertion that the distinguished physicians of the west had testified that they were human remains. About the last of December these remains reached this city; and on the first of January I was requested by a distinguished surgeon here to go with him on the invitation of the proprietor to examine them, and give an opinion. They had been erected in a high room; the skeleton was sustained in its erect position by a large upright beam of timber. At a glance it was apparent that it was nothing more than the skeleton of a young mastodon, (one of Godman's Tetracaulodons, with sockets for four tusks). The bones of the leg and ankle were complete, the metatarsal bones wanting. Most of the vertebrae were present; the ribs were mostly of wood. The pelvic arrangement was entirely of wood; the scapulae were present, but

somewhat broken, and were rigged on with a most human-like elevation; pieces of ribs supplying the want of clavicles. The osseous parts of the head were portions, nearly complete, of the upper and lower jaws. Some of the molars were quite complete; of the tusks, only one little stump remained, but the four alveoli of the upper jaw had large incisive looking wooden teeth fitted into them, and the lower jaw supplied to correspond. The cranium was entirely wanting from the lower margin of the orbits, back; but a raw-hide cranium was fitted on, which was much more becoming to the animal in his new capacity than the old one would have been.

The artificial construction was principally in the pelvis and head; and take it as thus built up, with its half human, half beast-like look, and its great hooked incisive teeth, it certainly must have conveyed to the ignorant spectator a most horrible idea of a hideous, diabolical giant, of which he no doubt dreamed for months. To one informed in such matters it really presented a most ludicrous figure.

The person who had it for exhibition was honest, I believe, in his convictions as to its being the remains of a man, having been confirmed in them by numerous physicians, whose certificates he had in his possession; and having asked and received my opinion, he determined to box it up, never to be exhibited again as the remains of a human being.

The "giant" Carpenter examined could have been from Franklin County, Williamson County, or possibly a different location altogether. Regardless, we have a captivating first-person account of one of the "giants" that traveled around the county and was exhibited for money in the mid-1800s. It was a composition of wired-together wood, leather, and fossilized elephant bones.

Who should we believe: the newspapers or Carpenter? That's an easy choice.

Wouldn't it be awesome if someone could find a box containing the "gigantic Fossil Man" described by Carpenter? This historical relic should belong in a museum to help showcase the scientific understanding of the past in the 1800s. If someone finds this "untraceable" and donates it to a museum somewhere, we would be willing to pony up a hundred bucks finders fee and a suitable award (a much more extravagant one than the majestic leg lamp from the Christmas Story). Look for a box labeled "Skeleton of Giant" with crossed-out words.

West Virginia

In 1959, Dr. Donald Dragoo, who served as the Curator for the Section of Man at the Carnegie Museum, made a remarkable discovery. While conducting a thorough excavation of the Cresap Mound in Northern West Virginia, he unearthed a skeleton measuring an impressive 7 feet 2 inches in height. This intriguing find sheds light on the historical and anthropological significance of the region.

> "This individual was of large proportions. When measured in the tomb, his length was approximately 7.04 feet. All of the long bones were heavy."

In his book, Dragoo substantiated his findings by including a photograph of the actual skeleton, which conclusively established its authenticity. This noteworthy discovery aligns Dragoo with a cadre of university-trained anthropologists and archaeologists who have documented the unearthing of skeletons exceeding seven feet in length within burial mounds. Intriguingly, these skeletal remains often exhibit anatomical anomalies, adding compelling depth to the study of our ancient predecessors.

Conclusion

Several reports of unusually tall skeletons have been featured in newspapers like The New York Times. For instance, there were sightings of two 12-foot skeletons in Jeffersonville, Kentucky (The New York Times, May 22, 1871) and Barnard, Missouri (The Providence Evening Press, September 13, 1883). Additionally, a 13-foot skeleton was reportedly found in Janesville, Wisconsin (The Public Ledger, August 25, 1870), and bones estimated to be from a 14-foot tall skeleton were discovered at Etowah Mounds (The New York Times, April 5, 1886). These measurements are well beyond the typical range for humans but are noteworthy due to their repeated mention in reputable newspapers.

Several professionals have reported discovering large skeletal remains. These professionals are:

- Dr. Walter B. Jones, from Moundsville, Alabama
- Dr. Forrest Clements, the head of Anthropology at the University of Oklahoma
- Dr. Donald A. Cadzow from Cambridge University
- Dr. Byron Cummings, the head of the archaeology department at the University of Arizona
- Thomas Wilson, Curator of Prehistoric Anthropology at the Smithsonian
- W. J. Holland, Curator of the Carnegie Museum

Their discoveries include skeletons measuring over 7 feet, 8 feet, and even taller, some with anatomical anomalies. These findings have been documented in scientific journals such as Scientific American.

With this compelling evidence, we must be willing to delve deep into the intricacies of our past and carefully consider the potential implications for our future. By meticulously examining the evidence and drawing well-informed conclusions, we can uncover valuable insights that are essential for comprehending the present and charting a course for the future.

13

The Elongated Skulls Of Peru

But God gives it a body just as He wished, and to each of the seeds a body of its own. All flesh is not the same flesh, but there is one flesh of men, and another flesh of beasts, and another flesh of birds, and another of fish.

Corinthians 15:38–39

The History of Cranial Head Binding

The Peruvian people, residing in the highlands of the Andean region, are known for their profound cultural practices, among which cranial head binding holds a significant place. This ancient custom, deeply embedded in Peruvian tradition, reflects a complex interplay of social status, spiritual beliefs, and cultural identity. Its origins and practice are a testament to the Peruvian worldview and a focal point in broader discussions about ancient cranial deformation practices, including those explored by researchers like L.A. Marzulli.

The practice of cranial head binding among the Peruvians dates back millennia. Historical records and oral traditions suggest that this custom originated as a means to delineate social classes and clan associations within Peruvian society. L.A.'s work on cranial deformation, especially his questioning ancient practices in different cultures, provides valuable context for understanding how such methods served social and spiritual purposes.

L.A.'s research underlines that cranial binding was common to the Peruvians but was also prevalent among other ancient cultures, such as the Maya and the Egyptians. According to L.A., these methods often had a symbolic role, reflecting the perceived connection between the individual and the divine. For the Peruvians, head binding personified their spiritual and cosmic beliefs, aligning individuals with the sacred order of Pachamama (Earth Mother) and Inti (Sun God).

The Practice of Head Binding

Cranial binding among the Peruvians is a meticulous and highly ritualized process that begins shortly after birth. Children's still-shapeable skulls were shaped using cloth strips, wooden planks, and other supportive materials. The desired shape is accomplished through a process that is both an art and a science, requiring great skill and care.

According to L.A.'s studies, the purposes of cranial deformation varied across cultures. Still, they often included signifying higher social status or extraordinary spiritual attributes. For the Peruvian people, head shapes were deeply symbolic. An elongated head might denote spiritual enlightenment or higher social standing. At the same time, other shapes could reflect different aspects of personal or communal identity.

In Peruvian culture, it was believed that the shapes of the head could influence an individual's destiny and spiritual alignment. Rituals and prayers accompanied the binding process, intended to invoke blessings from the spirits and deities. Elders and spiritual leaders conducted these ceremonies, ensuring the practice was infused with spiritual significance. Natural materials such as herbs and sacred oils enhanced the spiritual connection and ensured the process's sanctity.

Social and Cultural Implications

Historically, the cranial binding had profound social implications among the Peruvians. The shape of one's head could denote one's rank within the social hierarchy. High-ranking individuals, such as priests and shamans, often had more elaborate and pronounced head shapes, reinforcing their elevated status and spiritual authority. Conversely, commoners had more subdued head shapes, reflecting their lower status in the social order.

L.A.'s exploration of similar practices in ancient cultures underlines the universality of this social function. His work notes that cranial deformation often reinforces social structures and hierarchies, reflecting broader cultural values. For the Peruvians, this practice visually represented social distinctions and spiritual hierarchies within their community.

Over time, the practice of cranial binding evolved to encompass personal identity and spiritual aspirations. Individuals might undergo more intense or prolonged binding processes to demonstrate their commitment to spiritual practices or personal goals. This personal dimension of the practice allowed individuals to express their beliefs and aspirations while sticking to traditional customs.

Modern Perspectives

In modern times, the practice of cranial binding faces significant challenges. The pressures of globalization and modernization have introduced new influences, leading some Peruvians to question or abandon traditional customs. However, a dedicated segment of the Peruvian community was committed to preserving this practice as a vital link to their lineage.

L.A.'s research on the persistence of ancient practices gives insights into how traditional customs can adapt and survive amidst modern changes. His work suggests that while the external conditions and societal contexts may change, the heart of cultural values and spiritual beliefs associated with these practices often survive. In the case of the Peruvians, this means that efforts to record and restore cranial binding are part of a broader movement to maintain cultural identity in an ever-changing world.

The growing interest among younger generations in learning about and taking part in traditional practices shows a desire to preserve cultural roots while dealing with the challenges of modern life. This relationship between tradition and modernity shows cultural practices' resilience and ability to adapt to new environments.

The tradition of cranial head binding among the Peruvian people is a complex practice encompassing historical, social, and spiritual dimensions. Rooted in ancient beliefs and customs, it has influenced not only the physical appearances of its practitioners but also their social structures and cultural identity. The insights provided by L.A. and other scholars offer a broader understanding of how such practices fit into the larger tapestry of human cultural and spiritual history.

As the Peruvians continue to navigate the challenges of the modern era, their commitment to preserving and revitalizing cranial binding is a testament to the enduring power of cultural traditions. With its deep historical roots and profound spiritual significance, this practice remains a vital aspect of Peruvian heritage and identity, bridging the past and the present meaningfully and dynamically.

Similar Things

Similar things are happening today in our culture. Body modifications are encouraged in many different facets of society for many reasons. We may not see head binding as the Peruvians practiced, but a lot of body distortion is happening today. In light of the rapid advancements in technology right before our eyes, as followers of Yeshua, we must thoughtfully reflect on the relations between technology and our physical selves. The Bible offers a clear ethical framework to guide us through these challenging issues. According to Scripture, our bodies are intended to reflect the image of God.

Then God said, Let Us make mankind in Our image, according to Our likeness; and let them rule over the fish of the sea and over the birds of the sky and over the livestock and over all the earth, and over every crawling thing that crawls on the earth. Genesis 1:26

We can achieve this by responsibly managing our physical well-being, finding joy in our bodies, and desiring to align ourselves more closely with the true image of God, embodied in the Lord Jesus Christ.

...or do you not know that your body is a temple of the Holy Spirit who is in you, whom you have from God, and that you are not your own?

I Corinthians 6:19

Correcting The Historical Narrative

In 2014, the discovery of elongated skulls in Paracas, Peru, peeked considerable interest. A geneticist conducting the initial DNA testing reported that the skulls contain mitochondrial DNA with mutations not present in any human, primate, or known animal.

The most recent DNA testing has produced remarkable results. The tested skulls, dating back 2,000 years, have been found to share genetic links with Europe and the Middle East. These surprising findings seriously question our current understanding of the history of human settlement in the Americas.

In 1928, Peruvian archaeologist Julio Tello uncovered a large and intricate graveyard in Paracas, Peru. The graves contained the remains of individuals with the most extensive elongated skulls discovered anywhere on the planet.

The 'Paracas skulls,' uncovered by Julio Tello, are an assemblage of over 300 elongated skulls, some dating back roughly 3,000 years. The uncommon shape of these skulls has fascinated researchers.

Peculiar Characteristics of the Paracas Skulls

As noted earlier, skull elongation is typically a result of cranial deformation, head flattening, or head binding. Yet, the Paracas skulls reveal unique characteristics that differentiate them from ordinary human skulls, raising questions about their genesis.

L.A. explains how some of the Paracas skulls are different from normal human skulls:

He suggests that the elongated skulls found in Paracas could have resulted from cradle head binding. "I'm afraid I have to disagree. The opening at the base of the skull for the spinal cord, known as the foramen magnum, is located at the back of the skull. This is unlike a regular human skull closer to the jawline." He goes on to mention an archaeologist who authored a paper detailing his study of the positioning of the foramen magnum in approximately 1000 skulls, indicating that the position of the foramen magnum in the Paracas skulls is entirely different from that of a normal human being, and it is also smaller. This supports the theory that the elongated skulls are not the result of cradle head binding but rather a genetic trait.

He explains that some Paracas skulls have very pronounced disparities in cheekbones and eye sockets and lack a sagittal suture. The sagittal suture is the joint between the two parietal bones of the skull. In a typical human skull, a suture should run from the frontal plate across the skull, separating the two parietal plates and connecting with the occipital plate at the back. Yet, in the Paracas skulls, it is often observed that some specimens lack a sagittal suture.

Craniosynostosis is a disorder where the two parietal skull plates fuse together. Despite this, Marzulli has claimed that there is no evidence of craniosynostosis in the Paracas skulls.

The Test

Juan Navarro, the owner and administrator of the Museo Arqueológico Paracas, allowed the extraction of samples from three elongated skulls for DNA testing, including one belonging to a child. Another sample was acquired from a Peruvian skull that had been in the U.S. for 75 years. One of the skulls was calculated to be about 2,000 years old, while the other was supposed to be 800 years old.

The specimens included hair and bone powder extracted by drilling deeply into the foramen magnum. L.A. emphasized that this method reduces the risk of contamination.

The samples were sent to three different labs, two in the United States and one in Canada. The geneticists were only informed that the samples came from an ancient mummy to prevent them from forming any preconceived ideas.

Unforeseen Results

Out of the four hair samples, only mitochondrial DNA could be extracted. One of the samples couldn't be sequenced. However, the remaining three hair samples revealed a haplogroup, the genetic marker most commonly found in Eastern Europe and is also present at a low rate in Western Europe.

The skull test came back as derived from Mesopotamia, which is now Syria; it is essentially the heart of the fertile crescent. L.A. says it rewrites history as we know it.

If these results remain steadfast through additional tests, it indicates that people from Europe and the Middle East migrated to the Americas much earlier than previously believed.

L.A. said that mainstream academics would likely challenge these outcomes by indicating that he is not a scientist. Nevertheless, he challenges any unbeliever to reproduce the study. Attack the evidence, folks. Get your samples, pay for the lab, and then show me your science. The complete lab reports of the DNA tests are available in L.A.'s book Nephilim Hybrids.

The findings also support the evidence that many of the Paracas skulls still contain scraps of red hair, a hair color not indigenous to South America but originating from the Middle East and Europe. It's about genetics!

Unveiling the Hypothesis of Extra-Terrestrial Evidence

The Paracas skulls have unusual traits, leading to the long-held hypothesis of extra-terrestrial roots. Many have hoped that DNA testing would verify this hypothesis.

L.A. explained that the DNA results perfectly supported the hypothesis he had before performing any testing. This hypothesis notes that the Paracas people are the Nephilim. The Nephilim, as depicted in age-old biblical texts, are the offspring of Fallen Watchers and daughters of men,

> I was looking in the visions in my mind as I lay on my bed, and behold, an angelic watcher, a holy one, descended from heaven.
>
> Daniel 4:13
>
> And in that the king saw an angelic watcher, a holy one, descending from heaven…
>
> Daniel 4:23

> The Nephilim were on the earth in those days, and also afterward, when the sons of God came in to the daughters of mankind, and they bore children to them. Those were the mighty men who were of old, men of renown.
>
> Genesis 6:4

This resulted in a hybrid entity. They are said to have been conceived in the Mediterranean region, where the Paracas DNA comes from.

Whether or not this hypothesis is correct, the historical significance of the DNA tests' effects is undeniable.

There are many others with extensive information on this topic. For a more detailed study, check out "On the Trail of the Nephilim Ep. 6: DNA—The Final Results" on L.A.'s Website. Some of the information in this chapter was gleaned from this video.

> Be on the alert, stand firm in the faith, act like men, be strong.
>
> 1 Corinthians 16:13

> And in that you saw the iron mixed with common clay, they will combine with one another in the seed of men; but they will not adhere to one another, even as iron does not combine with pottery.
>
> Daniel 2:43

About the Authors

Dr. Greg Hood

Dr. Greg Hood was born and raised in Amory, Mississippi. Greg, an entrepreneur, has founded multiple businesses. He and his wife, Joan, are the owners of TMS of Tennessee, located in Franklin, TN, where they treat people with depression, anxiety, and PTSD. Greg has also been in ministry for over 38 years. He is the President and Founder of Greg Hood Ministries, Kingdom Life Network, and Kingdom University, all based in the United States of America. He is the lead apostle at Kingdom Life Ekklesia in Franklin, TN, which he and his wife, Joan, established in late 2021.

Greg apostolically leads many leaders and churches around the globe. He is a planter of apostolic centers and has pioneered several apostolic centers within the United States and other parts of the world. Greg travels extensively, empowering believers to passionately pursue their God-given mandate, resulting in personal and societal transformation. His greatest passion is to see the Body of Christ come to its fullness within the Kingdom of God. Greg is driven with great passion to speak into the lives of those called into leadership to the Church, Government, and the Marketplace. He burns to see people become who God has fashioned them to be.

Greg attended Christ for the Nations Institute in Dallas, Texas, from 1987 to 1988. He received his Master of Theology in

2006 and his Doctor of Theology in 2008 from Kairos Bible Training Center in Waco, Texas.

- *Rebuilding the Broken Altar; Awakening out of Chaos*
- *The Gospel of the Kingdom*
- *Sonship According to the Kingdom; Stepping into the Power of True Identity*
- *Citizenship According to the Kingdom; A Life of Governmental Authority.*

These books are also available in other languages.

Greg and Joan have been married for 28 years. The Hoods base their ministry headquarters in Franklin, Tennessee.

Contact Information

Dr. Greg Hood, Ph.D., Th.D.
Greg Hood Ministries / Kingdom University
1113 Murfreesboro Road
Suite 106 #222
Franklin, TN 37064
office@greghood.org
www.GregHood.org
www.KingdomU.org

Dr. Scott Oatsvall

Scott Oatsvall is a highly respected holistic health coach, cellular health scientist, bioenergetic specialist, educator, and author with over three decades of experience in education and health sciences.

He founded Life Transformation 360, a pioneering cellular health and all-natural healthcare company. Scott is dedicated to educating and coaching individuals on achieving total health of mind, body and spirit. His extensive education

About the Authors

includes an AA in Education from Mira Costa College, a BS in Sports Administration from San Diego State, Christian Leadership studies from Temple Theological Seminary, and a Ph.D. in Kingdom Studies from Kingdom University.

Scott is also an ordained minister through Kingdom Life Network. As an accomplished author and speaker, he has written and co-authored impactful books such as *And 1... Experiencing the Miracle of Adoption – Finding the Adventure of Saying Yes to God*, and *Finding God in the Middle of the Food Wars*, (co-written with Dr. Francis Myles).

Scott is also the distinguished host of *The Coach's Health Show*.

Scott resides in Franklin, TN, with his wife, Gwen, and their six children. Outside of his professional endeavors, he and his wife are devoted founders of 147 Team Ministries—a charitable organization that serves underprivileged, vulnerable, and at-risk children throughout the US and globally.

Contact Information

354 Downs Blvd
Suite 108
Franklin TN 37064

coach@LT360.com
www.LT360.com

Previous Work

Dr. Greg Hood

Praise for: *Sonship According to the Kingdom*

Sadly, many believers never come to a true understanding of who they really are in Christ. Paul rebuked the Corinthians for acting like mere humans. We are more than saved sinners; we are new creations. As sons and daughters of the Most High God, we're filled with His Spirit, infused with His nature, heirs in His kingdom, and partners in His great cause. You *will* come to a greater revelation of this as you read Greg Hood's powerful book *Sonship According to the Kingdom.*

Dr. Dutch Sheets
Dutch Sheets Ministries and *Give Him 15* Daily Prayer and Decrees.

Bestselling author of: *Authority in Prayer, An Appeal to Heaven, Intercessory Prayer*

As I ponder on Jewels in the Lord's Treasury, that at times have been lost and must be rediscovered, I am drawn to three words that start with the Letter "I." These are not just catchy words or phrases, but rather character traits. These are: 1) Integrity... 2) Intensity... and 3) Identity... It would easy for me to add in some of my other favorite Kingdom "I" Words such as "Intercession" and "Intentionally" and others.

I have the honor of endorsing Dr. Greg Hood's book, *Sonship According to the Kingdom*.

Equipped to Be An Equipper!

Dr. James W Goll
God Encounters Ministries, GOLL Ideation LLC

Nations are in a crisis driven largely by the curse of fatherlessness and the breakdown of the nuclear family unit. The solution: reversing the curse through *Sonship According to the Kingdom*. We belong. We are His. We are not forsaken. We are not orphans. He has taken fatherhood responsibility for us. This powerful book, penned by my friend Greg Hood, holds the keys not just for a transformed life but for the power to change the world!

Jane Hamon
Apostle, Vision Church @ Christian International
Author of *Dreams and Visions, The Deborah Company, The Cyrus Decree, Discernment and Declarations for Breakthrough*

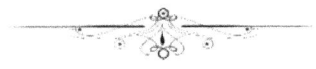

Previous Work

Sonship According to the Kingdom takes the reader on a thoughtful journey through what it means to be a child of God. Greg Hood demonstrates a passion to see people live life to the fullest. To do so, he points out, we must understand the resources at our disposal. Gone are the days when Christians can rationalize away a weak faith. *Sonship According to the Kingdom* challenges the reader to see tangible evidence of a life devoted to Christ. Those content with a mediocre lifestyle need not read this book.

Christina Bobb
Attorney for President Donald J. Trump
Author, *Stealing Your Vote: The Inside Story of the 2020 Election and What It Means for 2024*

Functioning in the miraculous power of the Lord, walking through test and trials and/or being used to impact the world with the kingdom of God requires essentially one thing. That thing is a revelation of who we are as the sons of God. When we, by the revelation of the Spirit of God, recognize our status with God, rejection vanishes and empowerment comes. My longtime friend, Greg Hood, does a masterful job of highlighting these truths in his new book *Sonship According to the Kingdom*. You will not be disappointed in your investment of this book. It could change your life!

Robert Henderson
Best-Selling Author of *The Courts of Heaven* series

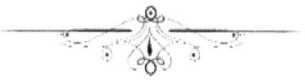

In the 1500-year-old classic book by Sun Tzu: *The Art of War*, we are reminded that for victory, "one must know their enemy...many fail to see that for victory, one must know themselves...." Dr. Greg Hood has hit the mark in his new book *Sonship According to the Kingdom*. He declares forcefully the importance of Kingdom believers embracing and living out their new identity in Christ. This powerful volume will unleash Kingdom potential in all who grasp its powerful truths....

Dr. Ron Phillips, D. Min
Pastor Emeritus Abba's House, Chattanooga, TN
Fresh Oil Ministries

This book is a must-read! I was informed, enlightened, and impacted as I devoured the pages of this well-written and very understandable volume!

I love the way Greg wove together a tapestry of Biblical, theological, historical, and autobiographical strands to present the revelation of the Kingdom of God, and its expression and ministry, in the earth through the sons and daughters of the Lord God. There are many places in the book where you will laugh as you are learning.

The heart of this book will assist the followers of King Jesus to be prepared for life and ministry as each one sees his or her identity as a son or a daughter of Father God and a member of His family.

Dr. Jim Hodges
Federation of Ministers and Churches International
Cedar Hill, TX

Previous Work

Praise for: *The Gospel of the Kingdom.*

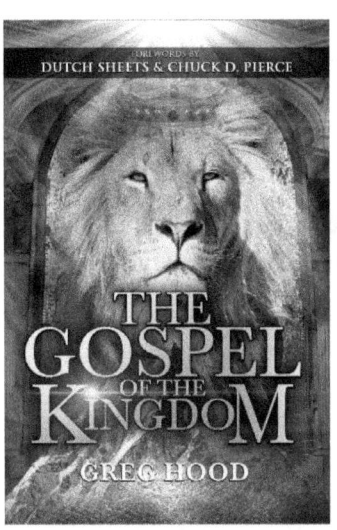

My friend, Greg Hood, is not only a teacher of the Word, but he is a student. Ever learning, ever maturing...as we all should be. The concepts and truth in this book may be new to you and that's okay. They are based on Scripture yet are just coming into their season. Kingdom, Kingdom Connection, Ekklesia, Apostles, Reigning in Life and so much more within these pages that will inspire you and encourage you and above all, change you. I encourage you to grab a cup of coffee, open your hearts and minds to what God is saying and doing, and take notes! Get ready to grow.

Tim Sheets, Apostle
Author of *Angel Armies, Angel Armies on Assignment, Planting the Heavens*
Tim Sheets Ministries
The Oasis Church, Middletown, Ohio

In *The Gospel of the Kingdom,* my friend Greg Hood gives us language that stirs our hearts with a fresh passion to see God's governmental rule manifested in the earth. This book will help develop in you a heart for that which God Himself is passionate about. Let it stir you with that which stirs Him, the redemption of all things back to Himself.

Robert Henderson
Best-Selling Author of *Courts of Heaven Series*

The Gospel of the Kingdom will revolutionize how believers live out the mission and mandate of Christ to change our world. Apostle Greg Hood brings a fresh approach to this vital topic which will empower members of Christ's Ekklesia to use their God given authority to cause God's Kingdom to come & will to be done on earth as it is in heaven.

Jane Hamon, Apostle
Vision Church

Apostolic and Prophetic voices everywhere agree that the church, the ekklesia, has shifted into a new age, a new Reformation. In his book, *The Gospel of the Kingdom*, Dr. Greg Hood challenges believers to shift out of a mindset of practicing a religion into one of fulfilling God's original Kingdom mandate to redeem and restore the earth. As God's earthly ambassadors of His Kingdom, we must grasp the authority and responsibility invested in us, and to examine scripture in a fresh light and understanding so that we can

Previous Work

cause the kingdoms of this world to become the kingdoms of our Lord and of his Christ.

Tom Hamon, Apostle
Vision Church

Dr. Greg Hood has written a very necessary book for the body of Christ at this critical time. It is an apostolic foundation for us to stand upon and will give context and order to our Kingdom call. *The Gospel of the Kingdom* has been written by a scholar who loves the word of God and has communicated in a fresh and direct way exactly what the Lord was sent by the Father to do and why we are being equipped, "For such a time as this." the Kingdom assignments that are before us will require binding the strongman and plundering the enemy.

Anne S. Tate
International Director of Prayer and the Watches
Glory of Zion, International

The Gospel of the Kingdom is one of the most important messages that undergirds much of our understanding of Scripture and the relationship between man and God. Jesus who was a perfect man and God incarnate made the Gospel of the Kingdom the essence of his preaching while he was on earth making the Gospel of the Kingdom the most important message Jesus ever preached and that he expects his followers all over the world to emulate. I am convinced that much of the body of Christ is weak because of a lack of understanding of the Gospel of the Kingdom. My dear friend Dr. Greg Hood's book completely changes that unfortunate trajectory by reintroducing much of the body of Christ to the Gospel of the

Kingdom. I highly recommend this powerful book for anyone who is serious about personal transformation and the transformation of culture.

Dr. Francis Myles
Author of *The Order of Melchizedek*
Founder: Francis Myles International

THIS BOOK! Here it is, an astoundingly simple yet profound picture of the Kingdom of God. Greg does such a great job of bringing the truth out about God's original intention, what He had in mind to do, from "...before the foundation of the world." This book clears up all the questionable things we have heard and been taught regarding His will, His character, His heart for humanity and His Kingdom purpose. It's a MUST-READ!

Apostle Randy Lopshire
Riverside Church
Clarksville, TN

My family and I have gotten to know Greg and Joan Hood, not only in a spiritual leadership way, but also in a personal way. They are true, kind and wise ... beyond their years

This book is an amazing read. Greg's wisdom and interpretation of scripture is so insightful and energizing! Everyone needs a copy of this book as a guideline for life and salvation! We are proud to know and love this man of God and have the utmost confidence in him.

Lily Isaacs and the Isaacs Family
Members of the Grand Ole Opry

Previous Work

Praise for *Rebuilding the Broken Altar–Awakening Out of Chaos.*

This book is as loaded with keen insight and Spirit-inspired revelation as any you will find. You would be hard pressed to find a book more timely and more relevant for the Church and the nations—especially America—than Rebuilding the Broken Altar. Sadly, many books simply restate others' teachings, simply coloring them with a different spin. However, it is refreshing when I read a book that feeds me new thoughts and information. Simply stated, I was more than entertained and inspired by Greg's book—I learned a lot!

Dr. Dutch Sheets, Dutch Sheets Ministries and Give Him 15 daily prayer and decrees.
Bestselling author of *Authority in Prayer, An Appeal to Heaven, Intercessory Prayer*

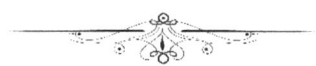

IF THERE WAS EVER A TIME WHEN a people needed to return to the Lord it is now. In his book "Rebuilding the Broken Altar" Greg Hood gives insight to the necessary process of recovering ourselves from the snare of the devil and experiencing the blessing of God again as a people. I would encourage, as you read to allow the Holy Spirit to stir your heart again with His passion for us individually and as a nation.

Robert Henderson
Best Selling Author of *The Courts of Heaven Series*

In *Rebuilding the Broken Altar*, Greg Hood presents a masterpiece of hope for the future of the church, for America and for nations crying out for a move of God. He carefully, Biblically and prophetically lays out a blueprint for revival that every leader and believer alike can work with to shift culture and engage the spiritual atmosphere to bring change. The word studies bring incredible insight and reveal the important elements necessary for rebuilding the altar of the Lord which has been broken down in both the church and in society in order to see an unprecedented outpouring from heaven, for harvest and transformation.

Dr. Jane Hamon, Vision Church @ Christian International
Author of *Dreams and Visions, The Deborah Company, The Cyrus Decree, Discernment*

My friend Greg Hood is known as hard-hitting, straight-shooting and uncompromising in his preaching. His writing is even more so! I love the way he boldly challenges us to break

Previous Work

free from old religious mindsets so that we can embrace God's kingdom plans. In his new book *Rebuilding the Broken Altar*, Greg gives us a clear vision of a restored church. With rich insights about the twelve tribes of Israel, he takes us on a journey toward the restoration of New Testament faith. You will be challenged and inspired!

J. Lee Grady, Author and Director of The Mordecai Project

Dr. Greg Hood helps us to understand the meaning of the time and grasp the seismic impact of the altar. I have had the privilege of Greg's friendship and the blessings of his clear prophetic voices. I praise the Lord Jesus for this valuable book.

Tamrat Layne, Former Prime Minister, Ethiopia

The bottom-line message of this book, God is not finished with you or America, but the church and some pastors and some of us in government need to get our stones together.

Rep. Gene Ward, PhD, Hawai'i House of Representatives

Previous Work

Praise for *Citizenship According to the Kingdom*

Powerful teaching in the last great worldwide move of God taught us much about our rights, benefits and responsibilities in the family of God. My Friend, Greg Hood, in his new book, *Citizenship According to the Kingdom, A Life of Governmental Authority*, takes this to a powerful and much-needed new level! The insights in this book are game-changers. Every believer should read this book.

Dr. Dutch Sheets
Dutch Sheets Ministries and *Give Him 15* Daily Prayer and Decrees. Bestselling author of: *Authority in Prayer, An Appeal to Heaven, Intercessory Prayer*
www.dutchsheets.org

My friend, Greg, has written a book empowered with great authority from our Father, bringing insight, revelation, and inspiration to equip each of us with the knowledge to live as sons and daughters of the Kingdom. It is more than a teaching manual; it is Holy Spirit breathed-upon, life-changing words. As you embrace them, meditate on them, and pray over them, you will walk in his freedom as a true citizen of his Kingdom, accomplishing his plans and purposes for your lives. Highly recommend.

Apostle Tim Sheets
Author of *Angel Armies, Angel Armies on As*signment, Planting the Heavens
Tim Sheets Ministries
The Oasis Church, Middletown, Ohio www.timsheets.org

When Jesus died on the cross, he took our sin with him and left the concept of religion behind. Despite efforts to eliminate religion from our culture, some still strive to keep it alive. In recent years, I have come to believe that many in the Church have chosen to follow the rules of religion rather than seeking a genuine relationship with God. It's important to remember that only the sacrifice of Jesus can save us, not any religious actions.

However, the Lord did not stop at giving us his authority. He also granted us the power to become prophets, priests, and kings.

Throughout each chapter of this book, Greg Hood instructs us on how to manifest the Kingdom of God in our daily 9-to-5 lives here on the earth. He emphasizes that this goes beyond the walls of the church house. While many of us may not be five-fold ministers, it is still a part of a king's life to lead and guide others, to pray and prophesy for the benefit of the body, not because we consider ourselves superior or more holy, but

Previous Work

because we have received the same care and guidance from others.

In addition to teaching us about citizenship, Greg also shows us how to be ambassadors for Christ and engage with the culture. His latest book, *Citizenship According to the Kingdom; A Life of Governmental Authority*, outlines how we can become influencers in the world. Although Greg has written other books on the Kingdom of God, this is his best work to date. I strongly recommend it as your next read.

Ricky Skaggs
15x Grammy Award Winner
Kentucky Music Hall of Fame – 2004
GMA Gospel Music Association Hall of Fame – 2012
Musicians Hall of Fame – 2016
The National Fiddler Hall of Fame – 2018
IBMA Bluegrass Music Hall of Fame – 2018
Country Music Hall of Fame - 2018

My friend Dr. Greg Hood's new book, *Citizenship According to the Kingdom: A Life of Governmental Authority*, will shift believers from an orphan mentality to a sonship identity; from serving religion to ruling and reigning in the Kingdom of God. It's a spirit-provoking read!

Jane Hamon
Co-apostle, Vision Church @Christian International
Author of *Dreams and Visions, Discernment, Declarations for Breakthrough, The Deborah Company* and *The Cyrus Decree*

My friend, Greg Hood, in his new work, *Citizenship According to the Kingdom; A Life of Governmental Authority*, challenges us to step up and take our place in God's kingdom purposes, especially in our roles in society and culture. In this present climate, where many Christian leaders are buying into the idea that we should just preach the gospel, Greg is showing us the other side of the coin. We are called, set and positioned by God to reclaim the foundations our nation was founded on, and our kingdom citizenship is step number one. Let this book stir you to do just that!

Robert Henderson
Best-Selling Author of the *Court of Heaven Series*

Dr. Greg Hood has done it again! He has written another excellent book concerning the prevailing theme of the Bible, i.e., the Kingdom of God.

He admirably weaves together the theological, cultural, political, and practical dimensions of being a citizen of God's present and eternal Kingdom. His explanation of the frequently misunderstood verse found in Philippians 3:20 impressed me: "For our citizenship is in heaven, from which we also eagerly wait for a Savior, the Lord Jesus Christ…." If the Body of Christ better understood this verse, they would not ignore their earthly citizenship responsibilities! How many times have we heard this statement by some followers of Jesus: "Politics is dirty, so don't get involved in cultural and political issues"? The apostle Paul knew and expressed his heavenly citizenship, but he also knew and exercised his Roman citizenship!

Greg explains how our heavenly citizenship calls us to responsibilities in our earthly citizenship. The main responsibility calls the Ekklesia-Church to be stewards and managers of the earth so that the will of God, which is always

Previous Work

being done in heaven, will increasingly be done on earth. This was the flashpoint of the prayer the Lord Jesus taught His followers to pray. As intercessors, we pray this Jesus-taught model prayer. In addition, as ambassadors, we steward and manage the implementation of the will of God on the earth. This is how our heavenly citizenship informs and empowers our earthly citizenship!

Reading this very readable volume, I walked away feeling like an overcomer. This book had a sound to it. It was like the author picked up a megaphone and shouted "Victory! Victory for the purposes and plans of the Lord God in history and on the earth!"

I encourage you to read this informative and inspirational book for your own edification and to teach others the vital truth of an advancing and increasing Kingdom of God now in the earth.

The Kingdom of God does not lose in history! I love how Dr. Hood expresses it: "Kingdom citizens gauge their worth by their influence on the earth."

Dr. Jim Hodges
Federation of Ministers and Churches International Cedar Hill, TX

Kingdom University

KINGDOM UNIVERSITY offers accredited and degreed classes in:

- Christian
- Kingdom Studies
- Business
- Five-Fold Ministry
- Government Studies
- The Arts

CAMPUSES IN:

- Georgia
- Indiana
- Louisiana
- Missouri
- North Carolina
- Texas
- Illinois
- Kentucky
- Mississippi
- New Jersey
- Tennessee
- Online Campus

More campuses coming to a state near you!

INSTRUCTORS INCLUDE:

Dr. Greg Hood	Dr. Ron Phillips	Dr. Barbara Wentroble
Dr. Dutch Sheets	Dr. Tod Zeiger	Dr Patti Amsden
Dr. Tim Sheets	Dr. Tom Schlueter	Apostle Bob Long
Dr. Jane Hamon	Dr. Alemu Beeftu	Apostle Regina Shank
Dr. Tom Hamon	Dr. Scott Reece	Apostle Kerry Kirkwood
Dr. Dwain Miller		

Kingdom University meets one weekend a month on a Friday evening and a Saturday. School year is from January-November. (We do not have classes in July and December.)

Register today by going to: www.KingdomU.org
Contact us at: Office@KingdomU.org

WE WILL SEE YOU IN THE CLASS ROOM!

Previous Work

Dr. Scott Oatsvall

Finding God in the Middle of the Food Wars, (co-written with Dr. Francis Myles)

Finding God In The Middle Of The Food Wars is a simple and sustainable blueprint on how to get healthy at the cellular level and become all that God has created you to be. The strategies and structure that reverse chronic illnesses and diseases are all contained in this book. Coach Scott and Dr. Myles layout a beautifully designed outline addressing the root cause of physical, mental, and spiritual health. This book contains the DNA of true health care and tackles our need to be healthy so that we can live our best life. This universal health plan

Previous Work

outlines a step-by-step formula that will equip anyone to overcome the 3T's that we all face...TRAUMA, TOXINS, and THOUGHTS!

And 1... Experiencing the Miracle of Adoption–Finding the Adventure of Saying Yes to God

www.ingramcontent.com/pod-product-compliance
Lightning Source LLC
Chambersburg PA
CBHW062226080426
42734CB00010B/2046